Stress Beyond 50

Tools and Wisdom for
a Happier Longer Life

Stress Beyond 50

Tools and Wisdom for a Happier Longer Life

Joan Vernikos PhD

Thirdage Books

Culpeper, Virginia, USA

Published by

Thirdage Books

2028 Golf Drive

Culpeper, VA 22701

www.joanvernikos.com

Printed in the United States of America.

ACKNOWLEDGMENTS

Thank you to all those who influenced my perspectives of what stress is and isn't, the astronauts and research volunteers who often brought me back to stress reality. You know who you are and I am forever grateful. It finally all makes sense to me.

Thank you to my husband Geoffrey who always insisted that stress is what I know best, his patience, support and thoughtful editing and my son George for consistently bringing me right back to task. You stuck it out to help me best reach the many who can benefit from a book written for those over 50.

I am grateful to Jack Boyd and Marta Hill Gray for their astute reading of the drafts, encouragement and valuable comments. And thank you to the readers who put in orders for this book prior to publication.

CONTENTS

Introduction

During my long life I've been a stress researcher, space medicine scientist, healthy aging proponent, teenager, woman, wife, mother, widow, NASA Director of Life Sciences, speaker, writer, consultant and *retiree* - someone who has experienced loss and sorrow, along with the joys of a life pretty well-lived.

This gives me an arsenal of life experiences and a particular perspective on stress research findings, on what stress is and the most practical and effective solutions to common stress encounters. Through all of it, and especially during these later years of my life, I've found that in many wealthy countries we fail to really discuss our stress, what it is, and how to deal specifically with the stress related to being older. With the hurried pace of life today, the money it takes to survive, and the increase in chronic illness, the pain and its costs, this isn't getting any easier. So, several years ago I wrote a book about it.

That book was called *Stress Fitness for Seniors*. Within its pages I did my best to highlight solutions to the most common life challenges experienced by people later in their lives. While the book was well received, it became clear pretty quickly (to me anyway) that there were important things omitted – both on the practical challenge side, and in the investigation of stress itself and how to relate to it in a healthy, productive way.

Why does this matter? We live longer now. One hundred years ago life expectancy for an American man was just 52 years – today that is considered more the mid-point of life. And stress today takes a tremendous toll on our collective physical and mental health. It also means an increased chance that we might lose our independence: that we'll need professional or amateur care at some point in our lives; or if we are the fortunate, healthy ones, we'll be compelled to provide it to a loved one.

Our increasingly sedentary lifestyles that I wrote about in 2011's *Sitting Kills, Moving Heals* have simply left us weaker, less coordinated, with a greater chance for physical and emotional breakdown. Poorly managed stress increases the risk of heart disease, obesity, asthma, depression and anxiety –it is the most pernicious cause of illness, pain and early death today. It also accounts for 80% of health care costs in the USA. In the workplace the experience and dedication of the older worker is less cherished than in the past, and retirement presents many of us with an existential crisis of sorts. By living longer, we also experience more loss than those younger than 50. Grieving and loneliness can be extraordinarily stressful when coupled with the other challenges of being an "older" person.

Yet with today's increased life span also come wonderful opportunities. We can apply and build on what we learned in the last 50 years to better our relationships, energize our careers, improve our health, and discover buried passions and dreams. *Stress Beyond 50* is about what you can do, starting today, wherever you are in your life journey, to more greatly enjoy the second half of your life by addressing stress more effectively.

I'll show you what stress is (and isn't), what the health consequences are of poorly managed stress, the likeliest types of stress you will face at some point of your life beyond 50 and the two main approaches to manage stress to your benefit, to become more *stress-fit*. At the end of each chapter you will find *Reflections*, questions or contemplations on what you just read. In Chapter 5 the *Stress Tool Kit* gives you a multitude of tools, many more than you will ever need, to help you keep stress within manageable and beneficial limits. However, the initiative to apply what you learn is entirely up to you. You must make the commitment. The next time something stressful happens get a little bit courageous. Feel confident that with your wisdom and new-found awareness you'll be better able to deal with it.

It's time to get started.

ONE | What is Stress?

One person's stress is another one's fun. Yet you mention stress and people instantly think 'BAD'. They cannot explain how other instances causing the same stress response can actually be experiences they enjoy or even need. How can that be?

A lifetime's career researching and living stress convinced me that there is no such thing as GOOD or BAD stress. Stress is life's stimulus. It gives you your sense of fun and excitement. This is the upside of stress. You cannot live without it.

Too much or too little of anything that sustains you, can, in excess, be stressful. Too hot or cold a temperature, too little or too much exercise, prolonged sitting or standing, too little or too much sun exposure, excessive eating or starvation, lack of sleep or oversleeping, too much or lack of oxygen, water, joy and sadness, unexpected events, are all stressful.

Did you know that merely standing up, as in getting out of bed in the morning, initiates a stress response? That's right, the whole lot – increased heart rate, blood pressure, adrenaline, cortisol, sugar and more. You normally are not aware of it because the response is so slight, but if you have let your health slip, you may be out of breath when next you stand up, your heart pounds and you experience a greater stress response all around. What matters is keeping stress within limits, to appreciate it for what it is and isn't, so that you can benefit maximally.

It all begins with what each stress means to you. Is it fun, is it familiar, are you healthy or is it a threat that triggers fear? You have gained wisdom as well as bad habits in your first 50 years. How you feel, your attitudes and beliefs and whether you take care of yourself determines how you respond, whether the stress is beneficial or a strain.

Dr. Hans Selye, a pathologist, first coined the term *stress* in physiology 100 years ago. He performed *post mortems* on humans and animals. He noticed that it did not matter what the cause of death was – all showed the same pattern of changes – the body's basic response to the threat of survival. We call it the stress response and he dubbed it the General Adaptation Syndrome.

Do you enjoy skiing down a steep slope or are you terrified? Sitting on top of a rocket to be launched into space would be considered stress for most but not the Gemini VII astronauts who had seen intense Vietnam and Korean War action flying hundreds of missions. My friend Bonnie loves bungee jumping. I am petrified at the mere thought of it. She and I look at the same stress from different perspectives. My brain sees it as a threat to my survival. In her case it is still survival, but she sees it as fun, as the challenge of overcoming it.

Going back to basics the word *stress* is used in physics and engineering to describe a force, pressure, tension applied to a piece of wood, metal or other material to test its resilience. The material suffers *strain*, relies on its flexibility to bend. It may even gain some flexibility. However, with persistent tension, the strain is too great and it snaps. In other languages the word for stress is *angst* – anxiety – which tells you immediately that the way we use it has to do with how we feel.

FRIEND OR FOE?

What makes the difference between thinking of stress as good or bad is how you view the situation. Whether you consider it an exciting challenge or are you filled with fear? How do you respond? As a child you may love riding a roller coaster though some of your friends may not join you. But when you reach 50 most of you may no longer think of it as fun.

The roller coaster has not changed. How you see it has changed. People are different and can view things with fear or excitement. You may love something or someone at some point in your life and feel hate, fear or revulsion at another. You may hate green beans when you are young but learn to love them later in life. You are also wiser. You can let go, laugh away what used to stress you.

In my early days with NASA in the 1960s I met the airplane test pilots at Dryden Research Center in Southern California. They were testing concepts of a remotely piloted vehicle (RPV) flown by a pilot on the ground as well as a pilot onboard. This was the early days of Unmanned Aerial

Vehicles (UAV) now known as drones. They were designed to be used not only in war zones but to help recovery efforts with supplies in otherwise inaccessible places such as after hurricanes, earthquakes and tsunamis.

The pilot on the ground did not want to crash this one-of-a-kind expensive technology. Another pilot was therefore in the vehicle who could take over in absolute emergency. I thought this was a great opportunity to measure stress levels. Who was more stressed the fellow on the ground or the one in the flight seat? After explaining that I needed a donation of urine from them in order to measure stress hormones, they stood up and thanked me, and one of them, Bill Dana, asked, "Little lady, why would I want to know if I was stressed?"

As I headed back home empty-handed, I realized I had just received my first lesson on good and bad stress and how these extraordinary men faced death in their jobs. What seemed a stress to me was a job to them. To be successful at what they did, they *needed to believe they were in control.* Worrying whether they were stressed would interfere with their performance.

Several years later I had the opportunity to measure cortisol in a group of men doing what I thought would be an extremely stressful job. Three pilots flew solo flights on U-2 planes out of NASA's Ames Research Center, in California. They did this three times a week for an ecological survey program flying over the Chesapeake Bay. Fifteen years earlier these same pilots had been flying spy missions, as Gary Powers had done when he was caught and downed over the Soviet Union. Each flight now lasted about 2 hr 25 min. At altitudes beyond 60,000 feet, they wore pressure suits and breathed 100% oxygen. Their feet were cold and their heads hot as they got closer to the sun. They had to recalculate and re-adjust fuel distribution in the plane to avoid stalling and were pleased if they only stalled about eight times per flight. To top it off, they had to photograph the terrain using a periscope camera attached through a hole in the floor of the plane. After all, that was the primary reason for their being up there.

A highly stressful experience one would have thought. But not only was their cortisol not increased, much like the Gemini astronauts, it was even lower than when they were on the ground. The only time one of them showed a response was on a day when there were unexpected strong crosswinds and a downdraft on landing. This reinforced the evidence that learning to believe they were in control meant they were not simply reacting to stress but actively suppressing their response. As Stanford psychologist Kelly McGonigal (2015) recently noted "stress is only harmful when you believe it is".

THRILL SEEKERS

Stress can be fun. It is part of the human make-up deliberately to seek the high that comes when stress hormones race through your body. For a baby, the thrill may come from defying gravity by taking its first steps and running helter-skelter across the room. As we grow up, it may be getting behind the wheel of our first car, revving up a powerful motor-bike, taking a ride on that roller-coaster, bungee jumping, sky-diving, surfing, skiing, rollerblading or snow-boarding, not to mention ski-jumping or diving from a high board into a pool. As we get a little older we may get our thrills from being a workaholic. Accomplishing the work, excelling, performing, is the workaholic's challenge for survival.

From a very early age why do we all enjoy being scared by horror or action movies? Why are action-packed video-games so popular? This is a way of seeking a high without exposure to real danger. Do we respond to these stresses? You bet we do. With beating heart, increased pressure, rapid shallow breathing of excitement it gives us a thrill. We survive danger. Any physical challenge, from mountain climbing and cave exploring to walking 60 miles to raise money for a charity, brings its own physical and emotional reward. It is by seeking new challenges, testing ourselves, that we push our limits and grow.

I decided in my early 40s to make the effort to learn how to ski so that I could take my children up to the slopes. We could then all enjoy the experience together. I went to Squaw Valley on a weekday on my own to get a head-start. Half way through the class, the Austrian instructor pulled me aside to return my ticket. "I cannot take this from you" said he. "There is no hope." Did I learn to ski? Enough to ski down the mountain. I did it by signing up the children for classes and following them at a slight distance. At 58, I learned how to play tennis which I love. With the roaring encouragement of the neighbors I learned how to ride a bicycle at 65!

Thrill is also inevitably tinged with some degree of fear. Any risk to survival is. Great actors know the feeling well when they step on the stage. Overcoming the fear element is what gives us our sense of control. However, too much fear overwhelms.

We freeze. We are paralyzed with *fright,* with apprehension and anxiety, unable to act, petrified— turned into stone.

Some go beyond the stage of a mere thrill and risk their lives or, at the very least, break their bones. Evil Knievel used his motorcycle for incredible stunt jumps. Chuck Yaeger broke the sound barrier in an airplane. The list of people who have pushed out the barriers is endless. Holger Ursin, at the University of Bergen in Norway, did a classic study with volunteers recruited to parachute jump out of an airplane. On their first jump, they showed a massive stress response. Though the stress of jumping had not changed, the response diminished with each successive jump. As the sense of accomplishment and control grew, their fear subsided, and their sense of elation increased.

Thrill-seeking challenges our limits. Our brain perceives it as a stress, and our body responds to this stress, until the brain learns that the threat is controllable. We survive.

One of the greatest thrills of all is to leave the bounds of Mother Earth. Many of us, as children, have gazed at the stars, wondered what lies out there and dreamed of going to the Moon and beyond. Many are applying to go to Mars one-way! Thousands have applied to train as astronauts or cosmonauts over the last 55 years, though very few are selected. The 550 who have flown in space so far are enraptured by the experience. Suddenly liberated from the pull of gravity, they enter a realm of euphoria. They look down at Earth, admire its beauty and feel awed by our smallness in the grand scheme of the Universe.

Those who landed on the Moon had a unique experience. But those who circled the Moon told me they felt a sense of loss and depression when they were on its dark side. They could no longer see Earth and felt separated from it. Suddenly, thrill had turned to the stress of loss. But why do all astronauts want to keep going back into space? US astronaut John Blaha, who commanded Columbia in the STS-58 Spacelab Life Science Mission (SLS-2) as it orbited the Earth in 1993, called going into space "a buzz." Professor Vincent, the French neurologist, calls it an addiction. Are thrill seekers addicts? They may well be. Certainly the brain networks and chemical transmitters involved in addiction are the same as those involved in the stress response.

Some of us become addicted to training for a marathon, biking long distances or going to the gym for our dose of stress. Yes, exercise is a stress. We use it to stress ourselves, our muscles, heart. Dr. Joe Mercola, an osteopathic physician with a highly popular alternative-health website, says "ideally, you want to do a variety of exercises and avoid doing the same ones all the time as this will not provide your body with the variety of stresses it needs to continuously adapt and improve."

We exercise repeatedly but with variety in order to get better. We make a habit of going to the gym at the same time or running the same route. Our approach to stress should be the same as to exercise. Yet we can get stuck in stress. For a happier longer life, we need to consciously acquire the wisdom to use stress just like exercise. Our goal is to "adapt and improve" in the way we deal with stress; to react to stress in an effective standard way that we have made a habit through training.

When I first arrived at NASA's Ames Research Center in California, I was impressed by the huge wind-tunnels. They were used to test the resilience of airplane frames to wind forces to test their ability to withstand the strain.

Humans are no different. We respond to stress such as changes in our environment – fire, flood, burglary –or we generate the stress in the gym or in our mind – what if I am late to work tomorrow? Get laid off? Or worse?

IT'S ALL ABOUT THE BRAIN

I think of stress as beginning with a trigger, a spark, a change, a thought, a challenge. The response may be a short beneficial protective reaction like pulling back your hand from a flame or a massive uncontrolled counterproductive outpouring of hormones that result in destructive oxidative stress and inflammation. That's right, you literally burn up as excessive stress piles up; we call it *burn-out.*

OUR CAVEMAN GENES

What you should realize right away is that the genes you inherited are the same as those of our caveman ancestors. They have been responding, in exactly the same way for thousands of years. What has changed is the nature of the stress. We are no longer chased by tigers or a hostile tribe with spears – well almost. We may be chased by a saber-toothed boss or stuck in morning traffic. What has also changed is to what extent our ability to respond and bounce back has adapted to modern living.

In other words, *stress is brought on by an event, a change, a thought, perceived as a demand, a threat that triggers fear which pushes the body to respond beyond its normal comfort limits.*

Perceived is the key word here, for the event itself is less important than the way it is interpreted. Here is where wisdom comes in.

STRESS IS A CHALLENGE – A STIMULUS

The initial response to stress is beneficial and essential. It has positive effects such as spurring motivation and awareness, alertness and a sense of urgency to face challenging situations. Steps include anticipation, excitement, apprehension and mild anxiety. Stress is your body's reaction to an event that stimulates you. When you encounter such an event, adrenaline, a stimulant hormone is released into your blood stream. Along with other hormones, adrenaline produces a number of changes which are intended to be protective, enabling strength, better performance that reinforces the exhilarating experience. This set of involuntary physiological changes is the *fight-or-flight response* described by Walter Cannon. Crucial to the survival of our ancestors, it prepares our body for a physical reaction to a threat. Failure is a setback. It feeds further anxiety and paralyzing fear. But a little bit of fear is not bad.

Sir Alex Ferguson, the legendary manager of Manchester United football club in their peak performance days, firmly believed in frequent challenge for his players to keep winning. René Meulensteen, the former Dutch manager of Fulham, was convinced that without such a challenge "you sink into fear." Consistently responding successfully to fear builds resilience. Too much fear for a prolonged time is a killer.

Our Stone Age ancestors in their caves were no strangers to stress, though their worries must have been very different from the concerns of most people in the modern world. Every day brought a new struggle for survival. They had to find food and shelter, fight off marauding animals, and escape their enemies. Natural disasters that happen today as well could strike without warning — a hurricane, a landslide, a flood, an earthquake, a forest fire, or a volcano blowing its top. Cavewomen went through menstrual cycles, had babies and menopause just like we do, though life had more physical hardships than ours. In today's world we are still engaged in a struggle for survival — perhaps less dramatic for most people but no less real. We all must provide food, shelter, social status, and a future for our families. Investors need to protect their savings from the vagaries of the stock market and the economy, and many employees live in fear of being laid off.

FIGHT OR FLIGHT

The purpose of the stress response is to generate energy, to prepare you to run or fight to survive. Over millions of years of evolution, human beings have developed *this fight or flight* response. For our remote ancestors, these were the only options. Coming face to face with a wild animal allowed no time for considering long-term strategies. In that near-miss, life or death situation a burst of energy was needed. Several systems were kicked into gear. One of those was a part of the brain called the hypothalamic-pituitary-adrenal system which released a cascade of hormones.

Adrenaline and cortisol swept through their bodies. They kicked up their heart rate, dilated the pupils of their eyes to see better, sweated to be more slippery, helped their brain with that split-second-decision, and increased glucose in the blood stream to give them that burst of energy. Physical activity helped deal with the crisis and clear these hormones from the bloodstream once the threat was over. This is their and your body's natural initial and crucial reaction to stress. Nothing has changed in this regard. We, however, today, do not always have the opportunity to respond to stress in a physical way. Do you see your boss as a fanged predator? An employee who has just been fired may well feel like punching his boss in the nose, but the impulse is usually restrained.

The stress response is useful, particularly in times of emergency – yet frequent triggering of the stress-response can contribute to a number of illnesses and symptoms. Any time your brain perceives a threat, whether real or imagined, your body begins this stress response. Much of the stress we feel today involves mental overload, bombarded with 24hr/day access to electronic devices. You may be worried about meeting a deadline or you are stuck in traffic and late for an appointment. Your inbox is overflowing. There are phone calls to return, a never-ending to-do list and somewhere amongst all this you need to fit family and God forbid... a life. Or you may remember the pain of losing a loved one.

Thought alone can cause the body to feel stressed. Performance can increase with stress but only to a certain point; when levels become too high, performance will decrease. Stress overload, too much or persistent stress, is associated with diminishing performance and effectiveness. Unrelieved stress can cause symptoms such as insomnia, chronic fatigue, headaches, inability to concentrate, general irritability as well as other physical problems.

Learning to recognize your early warning signals and taking steps to manage stress may protect you from a number of illnesses and symptoms caused by stress. Adding stress management to your daily routine improves your health, ability to sleep and general daily well-being.

LIFE EVENTS

In 1967, psychologists T.H. Holmes and R.H. Rahe at Washington University in St. Louis published a scale of social life events rated by how stressful they were. Data are from case histories of patients hospitalized for medical problems; the more severe the problem, the higher the stress score given for the life event the patient experienced during the previous year. "The Holmes-Rahe Life Stress Inventory" is shown below in Table 1.

Life Event	Stress Rating
Death of a spouse	100
Death of a child[2]	100
Divorce	73
Caregiving[2]	70
Move to Assisted Living[2]	70
Marital Separation	63
Jail term	63
Death of close family	63

Personal injury or illness	53
Death of a pet	53
Sleep Deprivation/sleep apnea	53
Marriage	50
Fired at work	47
Mortgage over $800,000	47
Marital reconciliation	45
Retirement	45
Change in health of family member	44
Obesity	44
Pregnancy	40
Sex difficulties	39
Gain of a new family member	39
Business readjustment	39
Change in financial state	38
Death of a close friend	37
Change to different line of work	36
Change in number of arguments with partner	35
Mortgage over $250,000[2]	31
Foreclosure of mortgage or loan	30
Change in responsibilities at work	29
Son or daughter leaving home	29
Trouble with in-laws	29
Outstanding personal achievement	28
Partner begins or stops work	26
Begin or end school	26
Revision in personal habits	25
Trouble with boss	24
Change in work hours or conditions	23
Change in residence	20
Change in schools	20
Change in recreation	20

Change in church activities	19
Change in social activities	18
Mortgage or loan less than $200,000[2]	17
Change in sleeping habits	16
Change in family get-togethers	15
Change in eating habits	15
Vacation	13
Christmas or holidays alone	12
Minor violations with the law	11

Source: Holmes & Rahe, "Holmes-Rahe life-changes scale," Journal of Psychosomatic Research, 2: 213—218 (1967). Adapted and updated by Joan Vernikos (2015)

[2]adjusted to 2015.New entries and/or equivalent value.

Each life event is assigned a value in arbitrary "life changing units" chosen to reflect the relative amount of stress the event causes in the population studied. Note that events represent a *change* of some kind. Stress is cumulative, so to estimate the total stress you are experiencing, add up the values corresponding to the events that have occurred in your life over the past year. If the same event happened twice, include the two scores:

150 pts or less *means a relatively low amount of the change and a low susceptibility to stress-induced health effects.*

150 to 300pts *means about a 50% chance of a major health breakdown in the next two years.*

300 pts or more *means the odds are greater than 50% that your health will be seriously affected.*

Things have changed since this list was developed. If you do not see items that are big in your life, you need to develop your own up-to-date list. Enter your stresses on this list placing them roughly at a score level based on how intense you feel that stress was for you.

For instance, death or disability of a child I would expect to rank around the 100 mark. Care-giving would also rank high. Being gay or lesbian was treated differently in the 1960s though the stress would certainly have been there together with the decision to come out. Fortunately, things have changed. A working woman would have faced stresses of work status as well as balancing work and family. A single mother's issues with child care have significantly changed as well in the last 50 years perhaps for the better. Having a child or grandchild in the military in a combat zone like Iraq or Afghanistan causes helpless stress. A returning veteran living with PTSD trying to readjust to a new life in the family left behind who are unable to appreciate his emotional struggle is very real these days. You will have your own examples. Developing your stress list will be valuable and specific to your approach in how to best address your stress.

Lifestyles and social priorities have also changed in the decades since this scale was first published — not least the value of a house and the size of a mortgage. Foreclosures were as important then as they are today. The concept of retirement planning was only introduced in the mid-1970s. Adult living communities and nursing homes as we now know them hardly existed and long-term-care insurance was unknown. There was an assumption that the family would take care of its parents. This often turns out to be wrong though it varies in different countries.

There have also been cultural changes in society. The pace of life has increased. People have less time to get more done. Electronic devices overwhelm their senses with communication 24/7. They are overloaded, mentally fatigued and stressed. Social skills including table manners no longer seem so important. Fast food has done away with the need for knives and forks. We have reverted to eating with our hands stuffing mouthfuls of food at our desk or even as we text. The demise of the sit-down family dinner — where families had the chance to catch up on each other's news and children had the opportunity to relax, learn and take part in informed conversation — has meant behavior in general is affected. Respect for others such as teachers and elders, is rare. Bullying and rudeness are on the rise. Coping with impoliteness is a new form of stress to deal with particularly for teachers and others in the 50+ generations.

Communities and families are becoming increasingly fragmented and anonymous. The stabilizing force of the family unit, its hierarchy and distributed responsibilities is becoming a thing of the past. Divorces, the financial burden of alimony with child support and the added burden of single parenthood and parental visits take their emotional toll. Care of children or bringing up the grandchildren just when you were looking forward to enjoying your later years brings stress galore. Care of parents fall by default on the 50 pluses and usually on women. There is responsibility to provide security to the children as well as an opportunity to rebalance the family. You will need to be stress-fit and resilient.

WHEN DOES A STIMULUS BECOME A STRESS?

There are five parts to stress processing, its response and how it can affect us. Broadly speaking

- the first step is how our brain receives and interprets the signal
- the second step processes the information against past experiences and practices in your data base, to alert and initiate
- the third step – the stress response.
- The fourth step involves a self- protecting mechanism that shuts off excessive response and
- the last step allows for recovery.

At first the signal goes through various stages in different parts of the brain. The *brain stem* generates instinctive drives for survival and reproduction. For instance, the fight or flight response to stress originates in this part of the brain, as does lust for another human.

The *limbic system* is situated on top of the brain stem and filters these instinctive drives through your *database* – a network of past experiences producing emotions such as thrills or fear, anger, desire and jealousy.

The *frontal cortex* is the area of the brain behind your fore- head. Sometimes referred to as the 'thinking brain', it allows you to analyze, plan, create and find meaning and purpose in life. The system is more intricate than this, involving other parts of the brain as well but this will serve the purpose for now.

Whatever has happened in your life has left traces in your memory regardless of whether you are aware of them. These patterns or feedback loops created by intricate connections in the brain are what shape your attitudes, beliefs, fears, and desires that you then bring to every new experience. The limbic system then takes over. So if for instance you were criticized for poor grades at school, you may react today with feelings of inadequacy that arouse fear and anxiety in the workplace. Or you may not learn a new sport or exercise through fear of failure.

Step 1. Stress – Brain processing – Perception – Fun or Fear – Helpful or not.

Step 2. The Data Base – think of this as your *box* – of genetics, confidence, how you think about yourself and your world, previous coping experience, health baseline – any of these can modify your response.

Step 3. The stress response, its magnitude – keeping it within limits.

Step 4. Feedback shut-off mechanism – resilience – oxytocin – calm, seek support, human contact, compassion.

Step 5. Recovery – a much needed pause to allow the system to return to normal. The duration of this pause depends on the magnitude and duration of the response and the resilience of the system.

1. PERCEPTION

How we think about stress matters. How we react to stress depends on our perceptions. Is this fun or a cause of fear?

This in turn is affected by

- attitudes – culture, age, education
- interpretation – is it a 'what if' something would happen?

- expectations – did something we were promised fall through? Unexpected or not being prepared for a natural disaster such as a mudslide, a basement flood, an exam or surprise guests.
- Predictability – is the outcome of your meeting with the boss predictable or one that drives your stress response?

Stress is only harmful when you believe it is.

Attitudes

A friend passes by in the street without so much as a nod. To one man this is a trivial event whereas to another it is highly stressful. He broods about the incident day and night, sleeps fretfully and wakes up night after night with a headache. But the incident was the same for both men. It was the detrimental strain (maybe fear of rejection) caused in the second man's interpretation of the incident that made the difference.

In my bed rest studies with healthy volunteers I found that reduced activity and the absence of frequent changes in posture were associated with a lower level of cortisol in the blood if the participants saw staying in bed as an opportunity to relax. This was the case with women. On the other hand, volunteers had higher stress levels if they viewed lying in bed continuously as confinement and helplessness as one would if put to bed due to sickness. This was mostly seen in first-timer men. This is a good example of how the perception of the same condition may or may not result in stress.

Looking at the positive rather than the negative things in life is something you learn as a very young child. People who trust others live longer. Attitude goes a long way to reducing stress levels. But if you are not one of these happy people, I will show you later in the book how you can learn to change your attitude and thereby reduce the stress level in your life.

Is it a 'What if' stress?

Perception is all-important in this situation. When faced with a stress, a virtual brain filter goes into effect first to assess whether the stress is real or self-generated – I call it a *What If?* It could include fear of being laid off, not being ready for a party or will it snow tomorrow? Will the car start? Something might happen to a relative in a war zone? And many such worries that have not happened and if they did you could not do anything about them at that time anyway.

It is said that 85% of stresses we encounter are *What ifs*, self-generated in this way. The thought usually begins with *What if?* It depends on how seriously the event is perceived as a threat that triggers fear and secondly the degree to which you can do something about it. They are most often worries that wake you up at 2 or 3 A.M. and are pure conjecture. You can delete them just like the spam on your computer. You have now instantly deleted 85% of your stress load.

Once your stress pile is reduced you have some options for handling the rest. At least the height of your pile is now more manageable.

2. THE DATA BASE

Think of the Data Base as your *Box*. Let us assume that you have now deleted that large burden of *What if* stresses that kept you worried. The most effective way to bring what remains under control is to screen it against your Data Base of past performance for *predictability* – same or similar stress encountered before – and *controllability* – how effectively did you deal with it? If both are positive, the response will be minimal. If never seen before, the data base is scanned for similar stresses and how they might have been dealt with.

If seen before but not dealt with effectively, this is an opportunity to upgrade your Data Base by coping effectively this time. Constantly upgrading your Data Base is a sure way to stay on top of your stress flow.

Old habits of dealing with stress may be good or bad leading to effective or ineffective behaviors that in turn feed into your Data Base. Changing one's mindset in order to change the way you coped is one way of dealing with the stress and improving the quality of your Data Base.

Whatever the challenge, the response depends on this Data Base of past experiences and actions. How did you proceed in similar situations before? If sustained stress puts a strain on your body and depending on how this strain is filtered, perceived and processed, and how healthy, confident and experienced you are, good advice is at hand. The Data Base is also where the magnitude of the response is determined.

How does the brain decide if something is serious enough to warrant a response? Each one of us has a different genetic makeup, has lived through different experiences, and has developed a personal database of memories and attitudes. The older you are the larger the database, good and bad.

The brain is an amazing instrument. It organizes experiences you have had in your life into blocks of information – data

– that it files away deep in your subconscious mind like memories. When faced with a tough decision, it automatically checks out these files to reason what to do next. This reasoning is like a subtle feeling, not always logical, that nudges you in a particular direction.

We call it intuition or gut feeling and it's usually right. Faced with a new and possibly threatening experience, you draw on this database. If the demand on your resources is predictable, the brain says, "I am familiar with this. What's more, I am ready for it. This does not present a threat to me. I am not afraid. I can tackle it. There is no need for a stress response."

For example, you are house-sitting for your grandchildren. You know that they regularly come home from school shortly after the end of the school day at 3 P.M., so their arrival at that time presents no particular challenge. But if the clock ticks around to 4:30 P.M. and they are not home yet, and this has never happened before, an alarm signal rings in your hypothalamus (Greek for lower chamber), a cherry-sized organ that sits strategically in the center of the base of your brain. The hypothalamus sets about mobilizing a stress response.

So, if you have a decision to make that you're sitting on, realize that on the other side of making this decision is relief, a whole new realm of freedom and possibility. Let go of your fear, tune into your gut instincts and take action. And if you're not happy with the results, simply take some new action and correct the course.

Baseline Sensitivity and Genetics
The baseline means where do you start out? Baseline sensitivity depends on your general state of health and your health

habits. Is this an isolated stress, chronic or one of many? How big a response depends on your state of health, time of day, do you get good sleep, nutrition, outlook, activity, mental or physical fatigue.

As with other bodily functions, stress hormones fluctuate — rise and fall during the day and night according to a daily rhythm — within a range of normal limits.

You may have inadequate time to recover from a previous stress as when you are giving care to a family member.

Within Limits

Normal limits are the range within which various systems in the body fluctuate when we are in good health and well adapted. For example, body temperature is considered normal if it fluctuates between 96°F in the morning and 99.9° F in the evening. Outside these limits it can increase or decrease by a couple of degrees before it becomes life threatening. Heat stroke results when the body's cooling system breaks down under the stress of very hot summer temperatures. At the other extreme, severe cold can cause death from hypothermia if the body temperature is not speedily brought back within normal limits. The body tries to stay within these limits by shivering when the weather is cold and sweating when it is hot. The normal limits of temperature can also be exceeded in cases of infection. We call this fever.

3. THE RESPONSE – HYPER READINESS

The instant result of the fight-or-flight response is highly visible, but inside the body the process is extremely complex.

As soon as the brain identifies an event as a change, whether you jump out of an airplane for a fun sky-dive or parachute in a war zone, it becomes a stimulus to the hypothalamus that activates two parallel systems that prepare the body for action: the sympathetic nervous system and a network of hormones, transported in the blood. Part of the autonomic nervous system, the sympathetic nervous system sends a stream of electrical and chemical messages to all parts of the body that help prepare the body for action. A power-packed cocktail of hormones — adrenaline, noradrenaline, cortisol, endorphins are only four of them — surge through the body for action.

In a split second, your muscles tense preparing you to pounce.

You have a burst of energy with a surge of glucose from your liver.

You feel more alert.

Your blood pressure rises.

Your heart pounds faster, your blood is enriched with oxygen as you breathe faster.

The pupils of your eyes dilate for more light and increase peripheral vision.

Your hearing sharpens.

You mentally focus on the event.

Cortisol gives you a sense of euphoria.

Memory is sharpened.

Endorphins pour out to blunt pain and give you an emotional high.

Vestiges from our cavemen ancestors are still present in this response. The body hair rises to make us look more threatening. Sweating increases and makes the body more slippery. Your blood clots more easily to reduce bleeding if you are injured.

Appetite, digestion and sex hormones are suppressed – all of them functions that are not needed for a swift stress response.

What happens at the hormonal level to produce this state of hyper-readiness? While the sympathetic nervous system goes into action, the hypothalamus sends its own hormone, CRH (Corticotrophin Releasing Hormone) to the pituitary, the master gland of the body, to call the hormone network into action. The pituitary hormone ACTH (Adrenocorticotropic Hormone) stimulates the adrenal glands to put out hormones that preserve the body's salt and water, vital to preventing dehydration and survival. One of these, cortisol, breaks down proteins into amino acids, which are carried in the blood to the liver to be converted into glucose for energy.

Adrenaline steps up the metabolic rate, instructs the liver to break down fats into fatty acids for fuel and convert starches into glucose for quick energy.

Cortisol diverts glucose fuel to the brain, heart and muscles by cutting down its availability to other organs.

It also constricts blood vessels and controls inflammation at wound sites. Yet another task for cortisol is to ensure that no energy is wasted, so it suppresses the immune system.

The pituitary gland pours out endorphins, the body's own opium-like pain-killers. Endorphins and adrenaline are responsible for the well-known emotional "high" that accompanies excitement. It is because of them that a person injured in a fight, the victim of a car accident, or a soldier wounded in battle may feel no pain when the blow lands, the leg is smashed, or the shrapnel strikes, and only feel the excruciating pain after the stress has subsided.

Stress hormones improve memory, allowing the result of the experience, including a record of how well we coped, to be imprinted in the Data-Base of the hippocampus.

Stress Response: Pile Up

Unmanaged stress allowed to pile up can get out of control. The ideal stress hormone response fluctuates between levels normally seen between night and day. Maintaining hormone levels high is usually the result of chronic stress and especially of allowing several stresses to pile up.

A single stress at a time is naturally turned off by the body's own feedback system within a day. A pile-up of unresolved, accumulated stress or continued elevated levels, result in massive, sustained outpouring of hormones which cause excessive damage to cells throughout the body; most critically through inflammation and oxidative stress resulting in cell destruction.

Excessive or persistent cortisol as in unmanaged stress has been called a killer hormone. But it only deserves these negative descriptions when the body puts out excessive amounts over a long period of time.

- Your eyelids may twitch.
- There is a risk of hearing loss and tinnitus (ringing in the ears).
- Headaches, insomnia, depression with an increased risk of dementia are possible.
- Continued high heart rate and blood pressure may lead to a higher risk of a heart attack and stroke.

- Sustained shallow rapid breathing worsens asthma and risk of COPD.
- Your throat and esophagus tightens, and may lead to acid reflux and GERD.
- Continued action of cortisol on the liver may lead to Type 2 diabetes, obesity and belly fat.
- Sustained high cortisol now suppresses the immune system and reduces the ability to control inflammation.
- Reactivation of viruses can lead to cold sores, acne or psoriasis
- Risk of irritable bowel syndrome.
- High cortisol destroys those same memory cells in the hippocampus.
- Chronically tightened muscles lead not only to muscle aches and spasms but to neck and back pain by pulling on nerves along the spine such as sciatica.
- Reduced sex hormones, decreased sex drive, can lead to infertility and erectile dysfunction.

It stands to reason that after you have dismissed your *What if* stresses you want to deal with your remaining pile. One effective way is to space them out if you can so that you allow recovery between individual stresses.

How Big a Response?
Even when the hypothalamus says "Go" to the pituitary to initiate this hormone cascade, the magnitude of this response is influenced by many factors. Women, for instance, put out more ACTH and cortisol than men for the same physical stim-

ulus. Your state of health, time of day, how well you sleep, eat, how active you are and what your outlook on life is, all affect the hormone response to stress.

Switching off

The system has a built-in safety valve that turns off the response as the cortisol levels get high. This feedback mechanism is extremely important for maintaining the stress response within healthy limits. As cortisol levels rise they act on the hypothalamus to block any further response. Excessive, relentless stress without allowing time for adequate recovery can override this shut-off switch with disastrous consequences as can be found in diseases and tumors of the pituitary.

Recovery

Once the stress response has been turned off, it takes time for the body to recover. The other part of the autonomic nervous system the para-sympathetic nervous system counteracts the stimulating effects of the sympathetic nervous system by slowing heart rate, lowering blood pressure, increasing digestive and gland activity, slowing down breathing and relaxing muscles. That is why you can activate your own body's relaxation response to help you manage stress.

During this recovery phase, systems that repair and restore reserves are rebuilt. Hormones like growth hormone, testosterone and estrogen go to work to rebuild muscle and bone in preparation for the next wave of stress. Allowing adequate time for this recovery process has an important bearing on the way we manage the next stress that comes along. Some everyday stresses can cause greater responses than others and so need more recovery time. It may take only an hour or so to calm down after being agitated because you had too many things to do and were interrupted by irritating telephone calls. But if you have just narrowly avoided an accident while driving, you may be so shaken up that it will take at least a day to recover. The recovery time for somebody who has actually been in an accident, even if they suffered no physical injury, may be as long as a week. Recovery from the loss of a loved one can take from 18 months to several years.

Adaptation

Given enough time between repeated bouts of the same stress, such as riding a bicycle on unfamiliar streets, the response gradually diminishes as we learn or adapt. Given time, a human being can adapt to almost anything. However, adapting to one kind of stress does not mean adapting to others. Adapting to the new cycling route does not transfer to other stressful situations, such as starting a new job, and certainly does not help much with your next visit to the dentist.

The human organism represents an integrated unit that is best when it works harmoniously. It is not stable but is dynamically changing continuously responding and coming to terms with its outer and inner environment. This dynamic form of balance is under constant change. Affected by external variables – climate, nutrition, injury, infection – and internal – emotions, pressure, anxiety, grief, elation. It therefore requires our constant attention and care. Stress can strengthen or weaken this balance.

The invasion by a foreign body is a stress just as an emotional or bodily injury. The immune system is the line of defense against foreign bodies such as bacteria or viruses that it cannot recognize and forms antibodies. Their encounter is a battle that results in inflammation and pain. Pain, the subjective sensation that something is wrong is the stress signal to reduce or stop inflammation; pain tells us some disturbance is afoot in the organism. Pain can become chronic, can be felt in the whole body and continues ceaselessly to alert that something is wrong until the inflammation subsides. Inflammation results as the tissue around the invader or injury becomes swollen and red. Blood rushes to the site bringing vitamins and minerals, binding agents, cytokines, interleukin-10, amino acids and cortisol to terminate the inflammation and initiate the recovery process. Recovery includes, among others, growth hormone to increase muscle mass and strength to restore metabolic reserves and telomerase to restore chromosomal metabolic function.

The stress response is essentially the body's elegant system designed to enable survival in even the most difficult circumstances. Stress is Nature's basic tuning stimulus that keeps the system responsive at all times. It is not the demon it is made out to be but only if we let it. Use the initial burst of energy to accomplish your goal, then learn to just let it go.

REFLECTIONS

These questions at the end of each chapter are to help you consider what you are already doing to best manage your stress, as well as identify ways to be even more effective in the future.

Grab a piece of paper and pen or pencil to complete these brief reflections.

- What things do you enjoy doing that technically are considered a stress? _____
_____

- Take the Holmes-Rahe Stress Inventory for Life Events that have occurred over the past year. What is your score?_____
See below for score interpretation.
Less than 150 Points: means a relatively low amount of life change and a low susceptibility to stress-induced health problems.

  150-300 points: You have a moderate to high chance of major stress-induced health problem in the near future.

  More than 300 points: You have a high to very high risk of major stress-induced health problems in the near future.

- Which high-stress life events (individual stress rating of 53 or greater) have you experienced during the past year? _____
- Do you have any of the symptoms identified as stress-triggered?   Y/N
- Do you appreciate how your perceptions affect how you react to other people and events?   Y/N
- From what you have read so far, can you now identify one or two possible solutions to bring your stress down a notch or two? _____
_____

TWO | Health Consequences of Poorly Managed Stress

Poorly managed stress makes worse just about every health condition.

A meta-analysis of 300 studies found chronic stress could damage your immune system. Stress may result in a variety of diseases, heart conditions, headaches, depression, gastrointestinal problems such as heartburn and irritable bowel syndrome, diabetes and obesity. It has been noted that reducing stress may have the potential to slow down the progression of Alzheimer's disease. Stress has been shown to accelerate aging and result in premature death. There was a 63% higher rate of death among caregivers than people their age who were not caregivers.

Your brain is bombarded every waking minute with information that demands decisions and responses. Too many demands can become overwhelming, especially if poor health has slowed you down. Hectic schedules can result in feelings of exhaustion, inadequacy and a lack of clarity in our work and personal lives.

Untreated, stress can seriously affect sleep, work performance, relationships and general well-being.

Which disease one gets depends on such factors as genetic predisposition, diet, activity and adequate sleep. The right diet can reduce the stress impact and restore balance to insulin, cortisol and other hormones. Adequate sleep can prevent metabolic disorders and obesity. Continuous movement prevents the chronic stress and inflammation from extended hours of sitting.

These all determine how healthy you are, which in turn impacts your ability to respond physically to stress. Americans identify stress as their number one health concern; 80% of healthcare costs are now associated with stress-related chronic illness says the Center for Disease Control (CDC). On the other hand, how you process the stress emotionally, affects skills you apply to reduce how much, how often, how long the stress will hang around. Will you just let it all pile up to an unmanageable level? Will you downsize your stress by managing your time, breaking up the stress with time-outs or calming interventions? Will you equip yourself with stress-relief tricks and techniques? Will you step back, assess the situation, seek help, rather than allow stress to burn you up? Remember, it is your stress. How you deal with it is up to you.

If you experience anxiety long enough your brain may become wired for it. Worse yet, some people are so used to feeling anxious that they don't realize there's a problem and suffer in silence. Chronic anxiety can lead to several physical disorders. You are setting yourself up for a crash in your overall health because your immune system is compromised; you have a heightened inflammatory response, raised cholesterol levels and blood pressure, blood sugar and hormonal imbalance with increased risk for cancer and brain chemistry changes.

RISK FACTORS

All stress, big and small, impacts your life. Unmanaged stress can make us feel awful emotionally, and worsens every other health condition. It may bring on a heart attack or make atrial fibrillation worse. It aggravates all conditions – obesity, diabetes, depression, gastrointestinal problems, cancer or asthma to name a few. If you want to avoid pain, the seasonal cold or flu, step up your stress management plan.

We become less responsive to change the older we get. We avoid change. We fear change. We flood our brain with worry of things that might happen. *What if?* Fear and worry become uncontrollable. Irrational fear floods our body with excessive defense hormones. Our brain is overwhelmed. Our body is overpowered, drained and paralyzed. All because we did not use the process described in the previous chapter to contain the stress, to manage it within limits but allowed it to get out of hand. Perhaps we *perceived* the stress – real or imaginary – with fear, as a threat to our survival. Fear can freeze, paralyze.

New research at Yale shows that everyday emotional stress is a trigger for the growth of tumors. My very first research project involved studying whether stress played a role in tumor growth. I injected ACTH, a prime stress hormone that normally stimulates cortisol secretion, into rats that already had a few tumor cells injected in their leg. Within a week, the tumor size of the injected rats grew to a golf-ball sized lump as compared to those that had not received ACTH. Stress seems to open up pathways for the spread of cancerous mutations even if located in different cells.

Premature death has also been linked to stress. A study looked at the health effects of stress by studying elderly caregivers – people who are naturally under a great deal of stress— looking after their spouses. It found that the caregivers had a 63% higher rate of death than people their age who were not caregivers.

Feeling stressed is becoming the norm. Feeling or being well or healthy is not merely the absence of illness or disability. It is bodily, emotional, spiritual and social balance. Health is being in balance; unhealthy is being off balance. Managing stress – reducing stress or avoiding it – is therefore a priority for being healthy and feeling well.

LEARN HOW TO MANAGE STRESS

"A funny thing happened on the way to space. I learned how to live better, more happily here on Earth. Over time I learned to anticipate problems in order to prevent them and how to respond effectively in critical situations. I learned how to neutralize fear, how to stay focused and how to succeed. In space attitude refers to orientation, which direction your vehicle is pointing relative to the Sun, Earth and other spacecraft. If you lose control of your attitude, two things happen: vehicle starts to spin, disorienting everyone onboard. It also strays from its course which could mean the difference between life and death.

> In my experience, something similar happens on Earth. Ultimately, I don't determine whether I arrive at the desired professional destination. The same variables are not of my control There's really one thing that I can control – my attitude during the journey which is what keeps me feeling steady and stable and whether they are headed in that direction. So, I consciously remain focused if because losing attitude would be far worse than not acting on my goal." Wise words of Col.Chris Hadfield, in *An Astronaut's Guide to Life on Earth: What going into space taught me about ingenuity, determination and being prepared for everything, 2013.*

GENETICS

Genetics do not seem to play a role in how much you respond to stress but rather play a significant role in predisposing you to a particular condition. A recent study (Kaliman et al. 2014) in persons who meditated regularly, showed that when they were exposed to a stressful situation, their genes and hormones that flare up in stress remained quiet – signs of healthy resilience that can lead to longer life. They did not have better genes, just better ability to regulate how the genes reacted.

Yet if there is a history of high blood pressure in your family, a high-salt diet coupled with stress will bring this complaint on sooner. On the other hand a low-salt diet, an active life and keeping your cool may prevent it from ever happening. High blood pressure may in turn lead to a heart attack, congestive heart failure or a stroke. Does diabetes, breast cancer or longevity run in your family? There might be a 20% chance that you have similar tendencies. It does not mean you will get whatever ran in your family; it just means that you may want to take special care along these lines. These days genetic profiling can tell you a lot about your predisposition.

However, how you respond to stress can be affected by your genetic predisposition as well. In the early 80s while studying human volunteers lying in bed continuously I measured their hormone response – the changes of a number of hormones in their blood – to standing up from bed. I used lying in bed as a means of lowering the influence of gravity on their body on earth in the same way that the influence of gravity on the body of astronauts is reduced in space. We used standing up to mimic the return to Earth and measured the response to the simple stress of standing up.

Although all my volunteers responded normally by maintaining their blood pressure and heart rate elevated, I noticed that there were individuals in whom some hormones increased more than in others. This tendency was consistent with any stress. In other words, there appeared to be a characteristic fingerprint profile typical of the way each individual responded to stress in general.

I hypothesized that this preferential way of responding to stress reflected the system – e.g. cardiovascular, gastro-intestinal, metabolic, emotional – that was their primary target of stress. For example, some people have an upset stomach or gut when stressed, some get constipated whereas others react with diarrhea, others get depressed, some react with a high HR and BP response, others with back pain. This suggested to me that measuring a single hormone or parameter in a group of humans would not necessarily reflect the response in all of them.

TAKING CHARGE OF YOUR STRESS

"I am so stressed!" is a common complaint. It means different things to different people. But in general it means that life has been allowed to run out of control. If indeed 80% of chronic illness is due to stress or even if it is a fraction of that, then starting with getting your stress under control should give you immediate health benefits. Where do you begin? Taking the Stress Health Inventory Test at the end of this chapter can help you get started on your way to recovery. It can help you become more aware of weaknesses in your health habits, suggest new habits, using the Stress Tool-Kit, guiding you to recognize and take more effective control of your stress. The more conscious you become of the risks of unmanaged stress, of the advantages of taking personal responsibility, the more successful will be the outcome.

Think of someone under stress, and you see a person looking haggard and old. Necessary as stress hormones are if within the healthy range, they are disastrous to your health when out of control. Consequences are both emotional as well as physical.

ANXIETY

Several parts of the brain are key areas in the production of fear and anxiety such as the almond-shaped *amygdala* and the *hippocampus* where memories are stored, playing significant roles in many anxiety disorders. These areas are also believed to be communication hubs between parts of the brain that process incoming sensory signals and parts that interpret these signals. They may alert the rest of the brain to an incoming threat, triggering fear and anxiety. Very distinct fears such as dread of spiders or of flying, create emotional reactions encoded in the hippocampus into memories and trigger fear and anxiety on call. It is these memory cells of the hippocampus that can be destroyed by excessive cortisol as a result of unmanaged chronic stress.

Emotions and Behavior

The hormone products of the stress response can bring on many mental disorders if present in excess or circulating in the body for too long. Cortisol, for instance, amplifies fear-related behavior, the last thing you need when defending your point of view.

Fear is necessary in the initiation of the stress response. Unfortunately the brain can generate fear without a genuine reason, bringing on a stress response that is unnecessary, inappropriate, and counterproductive. People described as "stressed out" commonly suffer from self-generated stress brought on by fear of something imaginary. They produce high levels of all the stress hormones, leading to anxiety, feelings of failure and guilt, worthlessness, hopelessness, and helplessness.

The usual reaction is to withdraw, go into one's shell and shun social contact. Why bother to look good, clean house, mow the lawn, take care of things? Who would care? Unless faced straight on, this is a sure road to depression.

In German and Greek, the terms for stress are *angst* and *anchos* respectively, which literally mean "anxiety." Mostly seen in women, what they have in common is unwarranted fear or distress that interferes with daily life. Some may go as far as to experience pain, nausea, weakness, diarrhea, upset stomach, depression or dizziness for no apparent physical cause. Have you come across a doctor who finding no evidence of any physical ailment, diagnoses you as if it's all in your head!

We have all experienced anxiety and recognize the symptoms: exaggerated worry about health, safety, money, missing a flight or deadline at work, fear of contamination and other aspects of life which bring on breathlessness, insomnia, eating disorders, indigestion, irritable bowel syndrome or migraine headaches. Other types of anxiety are irrational fear of terrorism, heights, elevators, crowds. I recently witnessed a panic attack at an airport. As airports have grown in size and complexity, they have become overwhelming to some. The lady I observed was frantically trying to negotiate the signs, trams, buses, escalators, queues and loudspeakers for fear of missing her flight. The airport personnel finally brought a wheelchair and took her to her gate. She promptly calmed down.

Living alone for a while may get you out of the habit of interacting socially. Anxiety in ordinary surroundings may be expressed as overwhelming self-consciousness, insecurity, lack of confidence, a fear of embarrassment possibly with a false sense of being watched.

We have heard or know someone with PTSD. However, this is not limited to battle-field experiences or recent events. Rape can also leave PTSD scars. Even with treatment, reliving an old but intense physical or emotional injury or threat can continue for life. Experiences like being caught up in hurricane Katrina in 2005 or Sandy in 2012, the Japanese tsunami and the ensuing radiation leaks reaching the US west coast, floods and forest fires in California, combat seen as far back as in Korea or Vietnam, the trauma of an earthquake or a fire, often result in symptoms. These include flashbacks, vivid nightmares and memories you prefer not to talk about, difficulty concentrating, sleeping, angry outbursts against loved ones even during sleep, a heightened startle response or the opposite of emotional withdrawal.

Depression and Pain

Depression is a pernicious and widespread psychological disorder exacerbated and sometimes brought on by self-generated stress. It can make people sleep too much or not enough, lose or gain weight, accumulate abdominal fat, have problems in their sex lives, loss of libido and interest in life itself sometimes ending in suicide. Depression and anxiety are more frequent in highly stressed individuals. People who reported stress related to their jobs, such as demanding work with few rewards, had an 80% higher risk of developing depression within a few years than people with lower stress.

There are 17 million diagnosed depressed persons in the US, and probably many more who are not diagnosed and never receive treatment. The higher levels of stress hormones in depression increase heart rate and blood pressure and may cause blood to thicken and clot possibly triggering heart attacks or stroke. Both coronary artery disease and osteoporosis have been associated with depression. Immune defenses are reduced. These conditions are not too surprising since depressives are by the nature of their disease inactive people. Bone and muscle loss, heart disease, and depression are especially common in inactive elderly people.

Medical scientists may not know exactly why, but it is established fact that depression can make other existing diseases worse. To complete the vicious cycle, the disease itself will usually deepen the depression.

Stress is often expressed as pain, both physical and emotional. Pain invariably is coupled with anxiety and depression. Brain imaging studies at the NIH have shown that many types of chronic pain show reduced gray matter as do patients with depression. Brain gray matter loss in the cerebral cortex may be associated with mood, emotional problems, memory and cognitive functioning as well as pain tolerance.

Heart

The aggravation of a condition that may start with a lesion or some form of irritation or tissue damage is characteristic of the way stress hormones work. What might begin as a localized small injury is aggravated by excessive cortisol that causes inflammation. Anxiety stress has been linked to a greater risk of heart attacks in both men and women. In the Nurses' Health Study that has been following women since 1976, those with the highest levels of fear-related anxiety were 59% more likely to have a heart attack and 31% more likely to die from one than women with the lowest anxiety levels. Headaches, muscle tension, lower back pain, memory lapses all round off their stress-related symptoms.

Similarly, a study of 10,000 British government workers tracked since 1985 found that those who reported a high level of stress had higher cortisol levels and a 68% higher risk of developing heart conditions than those reporting less stress. Yet it was found that the strongest connection between stress and heart conditions were found in men and women workers who were under 50 and less so in the over 50. The lead researcher Tarani Chandola said this may be because older men and women who still work are healthier because they have a better attitude towards work stress than their younger counterparts.

Type A personality has a higher risk of high blood pressure and heart problems. Sudden emotional stress can be a trigger to serious cardiac problems including heart attacks. The risk of a heart attack goes up to twice as high in the weeks surrounding a traumatic event like the death of a loved one. Stress can directly increase heart rate and blood flow and causes the release of cholesterol and triglycerides into the blood stream. It affects clotting mechanisms and aggravates the formation of aminoglycans (AGEs) that stiffen vascular and heart walls.

Gut

Gastrointestinal (GI) problems are frequently the body's tell-tale sign of stress. One of the earliest reported consequences of stress was that of peptic ulcers. People with stomach ulcers were promptly identified as being stressed and treatments were based on methods to protect the stomach lining and institute a stress-reduction program. Many years later a treatment was found when it was accidentally observed that ulcers were caused by bacteria and *only aggravated by stress.* This resulted in the use of antibiotics to effectively treat such ulcers. Similarly, stress can aggravate conditions such as Crohn's disease and irritable bowel syndrome (IBS). Stress is a common factor in GI conditions such as chronic heartburn for gastro-esophageal reflux disease (GERD).

Diabetes and Obesity

When you are stressed, and your body goes into survival mode, your adrenal glands release cortisol and adrenaline. Your pancreas puts out more insulin. Your heart rate and blood pressure increase while your blood clots more readily to protect you from bleeding. These hormones in excess set in motion a metabolic imbalance that leads to belly fat, weight gain, insulin resistance and ultimately diabetes. Brazilian scientists Macedo and Diez-Garcia (2014) found stressed-out women had a larger waist circumference compared to less-stressed women.

It has long been known that stress increases blood sugar. In fact, measuring blood sugar was the way to measure stress before methods for cortisol were developed. Insulin increases ACTH and cortisol secretion and sugar itself can increase both cortisol and adrenaline even in the absence of stress. Caffeine stimulates adrenaline and accentuates the secretion of ACTH and cortisol in response to stress as well. Thus stress, insulin, sugar and caffeine increase the stress hormones cortisol and adrenaline in a self-perpetuating, fat-depositing, fuel-depriving, insulin-resistance, vicious cycle. All of which leaves you feeling tired, fat and miserable.

Joan Vernikos

Skin, Muscles, Bones, Joints

Every organ of the body is a target of the stress response. One of the first places where too much stress shows up is on your skin. Tell-tale signs of unmanaged stress are acne, wrinkles, dryness and itchiness. In fact, unmanaged stress ages your looks.

The skin is the largest organ of the body. Not just wrapping tissue, it is an active immune organ. A support system with collagen much like joints, ligaments, tendons, bone and muscle, the skin has direct and indirect connections to the brain. As with stress, short-term inflammation helps fight off disease, but continuous inflammation produces oxidants that damage cells and is linked to diseases such as diabetes, arthritis and asthma. Cortisol breaks down collagen, so skin looks thin, papery, wrinkly, sagging and old. Joints wear out. Bone breaks down losing calcium. It becomes less dense and more fragile, contributing to osteoporosis. You are more likely to break a bone if you fall.

Muscles break down as well and get smaller and weaker. We need to keep them strong and ready to work to provide energy. But with chronic stress they become resistant to taking up sugar from the blood and are starved of fuel. We try to make up for it by eating more sugar. This, together with less activity, contributes to diabetes. Excess sugar is converted into fat stored in your belly. Normally, in response to stress, muscles contract to help you pounce or run away from danger. You know that from the tense feeling in the contracted muscles in the back of your neck, your frown, clenched teeth, tight fists and scrunched-up shoulders. Do you grind your teeth at night? Did you know that stress-induced muscle spasms are the most

50

frequent cause of back pain? If you want to know if someone is stressed check whether their shoulders are crunched up to their ears and if their jaw muscles are twitching.

Accelerated Aging

You'll age faster if you cannot manage stress. You'll age better if you can manage stress. Aging is the product of years of your life's relationship with stress. The skin is a visible target of stress and aging, causing thinning and wrinkling of the skin. Similar changes in skin texture occur any time you are prescribed cortisol or its synthetic analog, prednisone or prednisolone, or even when you apply a skin cream that contains cortisol or drops in your eyes for inflammation.

The aging effects of stress come right down to the cell level. Neuroscientist Robert Sapolsky's pioneering research at Stanford University showed how brain cells in the hippocampus responsible for processing short-term memory are destroyed by high levels of cortisol, which in small doses is beneficial.

Too much of the hormone cortisol secreted during intense or repeated stress can damage neurons, or brain cells, especially in the area of the hippocampus, the structure vital to learning and memory. At first the effect is reversible as new neurons fill the gaps, but after several months of high cortisol levels, neurons that die are lost permanently. Situations that lead to persistent high cortisol secretion, such as months of depression or exposure to combat, can cause atrophy of as much as 10-25% of neurons in this area. The brain shrinks and ages. To put it brutally, too much uncontrolled stress can cause permanent brain damage.

How long do you want to live? Much depends on the length of your telomeres. Biochemist Elizabeth Blackburn at the University of California, Berkeley, received the Nobel Prize for Medicine in 2009 for her work on telomeres, the bits of DNA that cap the ends of chromosomes in cells. Like the caps on your shoe laces, they keep your chromosomes from unraveling and damaging your genes. Telomeres also control the energy-producing machinery of each cell. Each time a normal cell divides, telomeres get a little shorter. When telomeres get too short the cell can no longer divide and dies. Blackburn identified telomere shortening as a key indicator of aging. Telomerase, the enzyme that repairs damaged telomeres, is reduced with aging.

Though it does not follow that reduced telomerase causes premature aging, there is enough science now to support that thesis. People with a rare genetic condition that reduces their telomerase production tend to show outward signs of premature aging and often die young of heart disease and lower resistance to infection.

Psychologist Elissa Epel of the University of California San Francisco teamed with Blackburn to address the question why people under stress look drawn, haggard and even old. They studied women aged 28 to 50. Thirty-nine were caregivers for a chronically ill child with cerebral palsy, autism or some other serious condition and 19 had healthy children. They were asked to answer a standard test to measure how stressed they felt during the previous month. The researchers then measured the cortisol in their blood and the telomeres in their mononuclear cells that are part of the body's immune system. Compared to healthy women, those who considered themselves most stressed had shorter telomeres as well as lower levels of telomerase with the highest cell damage seen in those mothers who had been caring for a disabled child the longest. Stress in these women seemed to accelerate aging by 9 to 17%.

Sleep and Alzheimer's Disease

Stress is a common cause of disturbed sleep. You are worrying about something, wake up in a state of anxiety and cannot go back to sleep. No doubt you will feel lousy the next morning and your looks will show it. But did you know that there is new experimental evidence that such disturbed, restless sleep may lead to Azheimer's?

Dr Jeffrey Iliff at the University of Rochester was studying how the brain's waste removal system – the g-lymphatic system – works (Iliff et al, 2014). Beta-amyloid which is normally produced in the brain, can build up as it does in Alzheimer's and clog the works if it is not cleared from the brain. Professor Mary Carskedon, at Brown University and others have now shown that disturbing sleep in mice as well as in humans on shift work schedules affects the normal function of this waste-clearing process which allows the beta-amyloid to accumulate. Early results suggest this waste removal system is most active during the first three hours of sleep. I cannot help feeling that the required change in posture such as lying down to sleep may be a necessary factor, just as sedentary lifestyles during the day may interfere with this detox function.

Immunity

A compelling reason to manage stress is to avoid the damaging effect of excessive stress on the immune system. The body's first immune defense is inflammation. Inflammation results from injury, infection or environmental pollutants such as increased gases, smoke, insecticides or preservatives. Chronic stress and excessive cortisol suppress the immune system and its ability to defend the body.

That is why the response to a cold may be a red and raw sore throat. It is also why redness and tenderness build up around an infected injury. Immune cells rush to the site of infection to fight off bacteria and viruses to promote healing. Daily we come into contact with some form of infection or toxin, but because we have a healthy immune response, we rarely contract an illness. Some viruses, however, like herpes bring on cold sores that remain present in our body in an inactive state for life. They flare up at times of stress. Almost all of us have had chicken pox as children but the virus stays dormant long after we recovered. It becomes virulent again at times of stress in the form of painful shingles. Fortunately, there is now a vaccine for shingles.

These flare-ups of viral infections are also evident in confined environments such as polar and space stations, submarines, airplanes, hospitals and nursing homes. And though we may not go to the Antarctic or a submarine any time soon, those who need to go into hospital when sick or injured with their immune response at its most vulnerable are more likely to pick up a hard-to-fight hospital infection. Similarly, it is not unusual to get sick after lack of sleep on a long flight in a closed airplane environment. Elderly people who have to be taken to hospital are more prone to get pneumonia than younger people, and often with fatal consequences. With increasing age the ability of most humans to organize an effective immune defense decreases.

Cancer and infectious diseases occur more frequently in those whose immune systems are run down. For a cancer patient, handling the stress of the disease is one of the keys to survival. A group of patients with skin cancer who took part in a six-week program where they learned stress management and coping skills and received psychological support increased their chances of survival and showed no recurrence of the disease five or six years later. The support of loved ones, friends, and relations is one of the most effective coping interventions.

Auto-immune diseases such as rheumatoid arthritis, Crohn's and lupus are believed to be brought on by a stress response that generates excessive inflammation. Auto-immune disease describes the condition in which antibodies manufactured by the immune system to defend an invading protein or toxic substance, turn against our own body as if they were attacking a foreign invader. In the case of arthritis, it is joints that are the target. In Crohn's disease, it is the lower intestine and in lupus, it is mainly the skin and other connective tissue.

Inflammation and Oxidative Stress

Just leave an apple on your counter and watch it grow old. First it shrivels and changes color and eventually it gets flabby and rots. That is oxidative stress at work. At the heart of it, excessive stress hormone outpouring in humans causes inflammation and increased oxidative damage just as in the apple. Simply put, the damage caused to a cell by oxidation is in itself a normal bodily process. It happens to our bodies and most living things that process oxygen. However, when there are disturbances in the natural oxidation process, such as the attraction of a free radical to another molecule in your body the results can often be toxic. Accumulation of free radicals makes mitochondria – the energy factories of the cell – become more permeable. This leads to the leaking of molecules from within the mitochondria into the cell. These leaked molecules trigger an immune response which, in turn, recognizes the leaked mitochondrial molecules as potential threats and destroys them.

A free radical is a highly reactive metabolite missing one or more electrons – it has at least one unpaired electron. These partial molecules aggressively scavenge seeking to replace their missing parts by attacking other molecules such as proteins in your body. They can cause damage to your DNA and other cell structures. Free radicals also have a snowballing effect in which molecule after molecule steals from its neighbor; the one that has been electron-robbed becomes a new free radical and so on. In doing this, cells may die as well as initiate or amplify inflammation. Substances such as Vitamins C and E may protect against oxidant-mediated inflammation and tissue damage by mopping up free radicals.

Though it may seem counterintuitive, cortisol, the hormone we all associate with stress, and its synthetic corticosteroid analogues like prednisolone, are widely used for their *anti-inflammatory* properties. Whether inflammation has resulted from a bee sting, poison ivy or auto-immune disease such as rheumatoid arthritis, the discovery of corticosteroids was a life-saver. They act by interrupting the cell-to-cell spread of inflammation thus allowing healing to occur. It is only unmanaged chronic stress where sustained excessive cortisol in fact becomes an independent *cause of inflammatory cell death*. External stresses such as pollution, too much sunlight, alcohol consumption, smoking, radiation, trigger the production of free radicals. Circulating sugars, primarily glucose and fructose found in soft drinks, are culprits as well. When these 'blood sugars' come into contact with proteins and lipids, a damaging reaction occurs forming AGEs particularly damaging, stiffening heart and blood vessels.

All types of unmanaged stress produce consequences through inflammation and oxidative damage of cell mitochondria. These oxidative stress mechanisms are thought to be involved in neurodegenerative diseases such as Parkinson's and Alzheimer's. Degenerative diseases like cancer, heart and lung disease, arthritis, fibromyalgia, type II diabetes, autoimmune diseases, eye diseases like macular degeneration are other examples of oxidative stress conditions.

The length of telomeres in mitochondria may be shortened by a variety of extreme situations. For instance, they are reduced both by inactivity as well as excessive exercise training. Oxidative stress and the reduction of telomeres in mitochondria are at the heart of the body's aging process.

WHY MANAGE STRESS?

A picture of gloom and doom is the common reaction to stress depicted in books and the media. You hear or read about it every day. Almost all of today's diseases — diabetes, high blood pressure, heart attacks, stroke, cancer, osteoporosis, arthritis — can be directly linked to chronic stress and our stressful lifestyles. Those that are not, are always made worse. I get concerned when someone in their 40s complains of an ache and dismisses it with "Oh, it's age" as if to say "I cannot do anything about it." Understanding the enemy, building up stress fitness, resilience is the best defense.

Uncontrolled stress kills, ages, cripples. There is no pill to treat it. Yet you have the power to modulate your stress response, to turn things around, to benefit, to pause between stresses and learn and adopt effective coping skills.

REFLECTIONS

- Do you fall asleep easily, sleep soundly, and wake up feeling refreshed? Y/N
- Do you often find it difficult to make decisions or concentrate? Y/N
- Do you avoid eating foods high in sugar? Y/N
- Do you generally feel calm, cheerful and in good spirits? Y/N
- Do you have chronic pain with persistent physical symptoms that do not respond well to treatment? Y/N
- What other ongoing health problems do you have that affect the quality of your life? _____ _____
- On a scale of 1 to 10 (where 10 is best), how do you rate your health right now overall? _____

THREE | **Stress Sources & Practical Solutions**

S tress is no better or worse after 50. However, both stress and you are different. Not least because you have become wiser and more experienced in the process of living.

Things that bothered you mostly in your 30s now may seem trivial. This book helps those 50 or older with the most common situations you are likely to encounter after 50, as well as giving you the tools to sail through them. They are presented here in the order you are likely to encounter them with passing years.

Babies, home and work were your issue at 20, 30 and 40. Fifties and 60s may be the best years of your life – peak career, earning, a sense of freedom and fun. Or you may be worrying about an empty nest as children leave the home, retirement, health, reduced mobility, tight money, care-giving, care-receiving and end of life.

What you took in your stride may now seem like hard work. You did not think twice about throwing a birthday party for 20 children squealing with joy but now you wonder how you did it all. You learned to balance work and life but now that may seem harder. Yet it is mostly you that has changed.

New types of stress will likely show up during this second half of life. Work may be more exciting as you achieve and are recognized. As a lawyer, you may be considered for that judge vacancy, as a teacher, for a school principal job. You may be apprehensive about moving up. Or you may feel stuck and going nowhere looking at retirement with anticipation. Life and family responsibilities change as well. Your parents are getting older. They may need help. Your grandchildren are a joy but live too far away. Or you may be caring for them full-time. You may be lonely or not feel appreciated. On the other hand this may be the best of times; you may feel a wonderful sense of freedom to do what you really want to do! Life is changing constantly and change can be stressful depending on how you see it.

Likely scenarios of the types of issues that gain greater importance are debt, a rising cost of living and medical care costs that mount over longer periods of time. As we live longer both physical and emotional health, as mobility and loneliness may be expected. You turn first to the Obituary page in the paper. Losing friends and family are more common. We cannot put half the population in assisted living facilities. Who will provide services, care and financial support? Where families were once expected to care for parents and grandparents, as done in other countries, this now rarely happens in the USA.

With the possible exception of the privileged top 2% of earners who are able to dictate their care circumstances, family and community living will need to evolve in tandem with changes in longevity.

Whereas someone whose lifespan was 50 years was lucky to see children married and grandchildren born, it is now not unusual for someone's life to span four generations. The social, family, education, work-span, retirement and healthcare implications of this longevity revolution including costs of sustenance and housing must be reconsidered. In addition to the possible need to care for a sick or disabled spouse or child, the care of aging parents as well as grandparents living longer is a reality.

No health-care system can cover all such costs. Retirement and assisted living communities will have to be rethought as should the concept of when aging, dependence and, for that matter, retirement begin. If we wish to remain independent for as long as we live, now is the time to address the issues that come with the next 50 years and acquire the coping skills to make the most of them.

Attitudes will have to change, not least with what is considered "old." When does one need to be taken care of and who takes care of whom? Retirement, in the traditional sense of sitting out your remaining years, just like too much sitting, is bad for your health.

SURVIVAL

In today's world we are still engaged in a struggle for survival – less dramatic for most people, but no less real. Natural disasters can still strike without warning – a hurricane, a flood, an earthquake, a forest fire, or an erupting volcano are all too frequent reminders that what you once thought was security, because you had a roof over your head, is no more. Hurricanes were not expected in New York City, yet Sandy's trail caused an aftermath of devastation beyond all expectations bringing us back to stone-age survival mode. Those with all their resources in their home were doubly hit.

Even in less dramatic conditions we all have to provide food, shelter, social status and a future for our families. Investors need to protect their savings from the vagaries of the stock market, or the malfeasance of crooked institutions and the Bernie Madoffs of the world. Employees live in fear of being laid off or having their jobs outsourced. A younger employee would cost less. A marriage may break up. A spouse may die, or take off on an extramarital affair – an expensive way to raise one's self–confidence.

Those approaching 50 may worry about the children's and grandchildren's education and future. Others may dread loneliness, fear of burglary or abuse, loss of independence or home, and the decision by others of confining us to an assisted living facility or nursing home until we die. Ever-changing information technology is leaving some of us behind and isolated if they cannot or choose not to keep up. Though everyone may be affected, we seem more vulnerable. There is the ever-present threat of a terrorist attack. Just like our caveman ancestors we too react with fear.

People in the over 50 age-bracket may fear being out of work because of out-sourcing. A younger employee would cost less.

Mid-life employees even if working for the government where they cannot be fired, find that their position can nevertheless be downgraded to a lower pay or reorganized into a lesser position. Later on in life, what does retirement mean and how will they cope? Maybe they are empty-nesters, relearning how to live without the children yet worrying about their future. Perhaps, the glamour of living with that partner has faded in the intervening years. Maybe a spouse or older parent needs full-time care or is worried about a fall. The balancing act of family work and care-giving looms large again but this time it is caring for parents.

Communities and families are becoming increasingly fragmented and anonymous. The stabilizing force of the family unit, its hierarchy and distributed responsibilities are becoming a thing of the past. Divorces, the financial burden of alimony with child support and the added burden of single parenthood and parental visits take their emotional toll. Care of children or bringing up the grandchildren just when you were looking forward to enjoying your later years brings stress galore.

Care of parents fall by default on the 50 pluses and usually on women. There is responsibility to provide security to the children as well as an opportunity to rebalance the family. You will need to be stress-fit and resilient.

STRESSES AND SOLUTIONS

A 2014 survey by the MIT Age Lab of several thousand people across the USA, revealed that responders in their 40s identified stressors as mostly related to juggling work with family. In their 50s, both men and women were most likely to focus on care-giving for an older relative or work-family-care-giving balance. The instability of family life, marriage, separation, divorce or widowhood and the underlying decision process were also major stressors. Moving on to their 60s, women's primary stress was care-giving, followed by work and money whereas men's primary concern was around financial issues, including finding another job.

What to Do About It

- All of these can be addressed by better communication of parties involved and honest analysis of each situation before it becomes overwhelming.

YOUR RELATIONSHIP WITH STRESS

The good news is that life in retirement need not be like this. A sense of purpose throughout your life has been shown to be a key ingredient to a happier longer life. All it takes is some early, pre-retirement career planning. Just like putting away money for retirement is not achieved overnight, so the mental adjustment to a change in routine, responsibilities and interacting more with a different set of social contacts—maybe your family—takes time to happen. It takes effort.

How healthy you are and how well you feel at 50 can influence how well you respond to stress. Anything that alters this baseline or alters normal limits and the daily rhythm of these changes will affect a person's responsiveness to stress. For example, the stress hormone cortisol peaks before you wake up in the morning. Cortisol increases blood sugar from the glycogen stores in the liver to prepare the body with the extra energy it needs to get going. Cortisol then decreases throughout the day as energy fizzles and remains very low in the evening and into the night to prepare you for sleep. Some stress-provoking event like exercising in the evening may cause a further surge in production that will interfere with sleep.

Both the high in the morning and the low in the evening are important for health. Morning levels that are lower than average, are often found in otherwise healthy but inactive individuals, as well as in the elderly, in children living in institutions, and in people with PTSD. By lying in bed or being inactive, the adrenal gland gradually becomes less sensitive to ACTH, the pituitary hormone that regulates it. As a result, more ACTH is needed to generate the appropriate response from the adrenal. In prolonged bed rest, this reduced sensitivity takes fourteen to thirty days to develop and is restored twenty days after volunteers get out of bed and move about. Decreased adrenal responsiveness is common in permanently inactive individuals, including those made inactive by spinal cord injury. Such reduced sensitivity has long been known to also occur as people grow older. However, it is most likely that this is the consequence of gradually decreasing activity over a lifetime, rather than of age itself.

What to Do About It

- Learn to manage stress in general. This is not easy but possible if your Data Base is rich in positive experiences and you can build up your self-confidence.

- Nurture your passion. Do you have a purpose in life, curiosity about everything and everyone around you, not just the bad news on TV?
- Spread out your pile of stress over time so that each becomes manageable.
- Take time-outs between stresses to allow yourself to recover. You may use satisfying activities that are unrelated to your stress; go out for a short walk, get correspondence done, return phone calls, walk up and down stairs to burn up energy.

THE FEAR OF UNCERTAINTY

Change, real or imaginary, brings uncertainty. Our first reaction to change is fear. Fear is a feeling and feelings can be changed. Almost every worry or reaction begins with fear. You misplaced your keys. What do you do? You search your clothes, the car, your favorite spots, you panic or worse the fleeting threat of Alzheimer's rears its head. You are afraid that you will miss your appointment or get to work late. You make frantic calls. You then begin to retrace your steps. When did you last have them, what were you wearing, where did you go and there –bingo – are your keys! We all do it, at every age.

The sudden loss of my first husband at 35 generated fear and insecurity in me. I grieved at how I would cope with two young children and a job. Ridiculous as it may seem today one of my main worries was who would take care of the car when it broke down? Soon enough I learned and had to plan my time, identifying sources of help accordingly. I got a new appreciation of what single mothers have to deal with. I was grateful for my job and my colleagues which I loved. It meant I would not have to worry about income.

Most people have some degree of fear when going to the doctor. Blood pressure and heart rate is always up. Relief of that fear comes from knowing the facts even if they are less than pleasant. Fear can be generated during a windy night that keeps us awake and anxious or an unusual noise in the house. What do you do? We all develop ways of tackling our fears throughout life, some more effectively than others but also differently at different times and as we age.

Probably the primary source of stress in men or women in mid-life onward deals with uncertainty that generates fear – fear of failure, fear of job loss or reorganization or fear of retirement. Are you more reluctant to say "No"? With retirement comes fear of loss of financial security, personal security, loss of home or partner. You may be facing failing health, vision, hearing. Fear of loss of independence comes with fear of the unknown that lies ahead. Are you reluctant to venture out alone or drive after dark or of being left alone.

The list goes on. Men's worst fears deal mostly with work and money, followed by fading sexual prowess. Women, on the other hand, emphasize health with money a close second. Since 50+ begins with late working life, progressing to early years of retirement and then extended retirement to aging. Types of stress issues vary over time as well as gender.

Fear comes with the stress of decision-making. We procrastinate. We have greater expectations of ourselves at 50+ than we did at 25. When you make a decision you stop procrastinating. You get off the fence. No looking back. You just move forward. A lot of freedom comes with that! The fear of failure may be *internal* or *external*. Are you afraid of making the wrong decision? Or *are you afraid of looking bad if you make the wrong decision?* Tony Robbins says "there is no such thing as failure. There are only results. You always produce a result. If it's not the one you desire, just change your actions and you'll produce new results."

What to Do About It

- Make a decision. Any decision is better than none. No looking back. Only forward.
- Seek advice if you need to put things in perspective.
- More time debating the decision will not help.

FEAR OF LOSING CONTROL

Fear of losing control comes at any age. Research that measured hormones in medical students taking exams showed that each one of us has a characteristic stress response, a kind of hormone fingerprint. This profile may indicate that a person is likely to suffer such problems as either heart disease, diabetes, or auto-immune disease at a later age — or that he or she is likely to be free of them. Typical behaviors often go with the profile.

Myer Rosenman and Ray Friedman, two San Francisco cardiologists at the Mount Zion Medical Center, coined the term Type A for persons most likely to have a heart attack after they noticed a lot of wear and tear on chairs in their waiting room not too long after the chairs had been reupholstered. However, the fabric was worn out only at the front edge of the seat, whereas the rest of the seat looked brand new. They concluded that since most of their patients were there because they had suffered a heart attack, or were good candidates for one, sitting on the edge of the seat revealed something about their personalities.

Further analysis showed that Type A patients were always competitive, achievement-oriented, and pushed for time. Fear of losing control in their lives was a major threat. Their calmer patients, classified as Type B, did not wear out the fronts of their chairs. They were quite happy not being busy and found that pressure at work was stressful rather than stimulating. They are those with many outside hobbies and interests who were more likely to adapt to retirement and enjoy it. Type A subjects were stressed when they were deprived of work. They were those most likely to drop dead shortly after receiving their retirement watch.

We hear much about job stress. These days much more is expected in the workplace from fewer people. Long hours, information overload, less personal interaction, and a stream of e-mail every day from colleagues just down the hall, have become common features of everyday working life. Type As may thrive in this high-pressure environment. Type Bs feel swamped, angry, and frustrated. We recognize Type As as workaholics, which is really a form of addiction.

What to Do About It

- You cannot control what happens but you can control how you deal with it.
- Identify what type of personality you have and how you respond to stress.

- Work on changing habits to allow yourself time to meet demands.

TURN IT INTO AN OPPORTUNITY

Losing a job in your 50s can be a devastating blow mostly to your ego because it was not in your plans. How could this happen to me? What if I had done this or that? Bear in mind any kind of loss is challenging.

Let go. Turn it into an opportunity. Move forward. Build your self-esteem and sustain your sense of worth. Develop interests outside work.

Dr. Ruth Hendricks, an avid athlete and healthy aging expert, was one of those who flashed through the stages of loss on being told at age 43 that she urgently needed a mastectomy. In her book *Race for Life* she tells of her reaction to the news after having been misdiagnosed for three years. "I wanted to scream, yell, hit out, rage, vent my fury, roll over, and die. Hey, wait a minute, I thought. I'm not ready to roll over and die. I was fighting to live and was going to fight this death sentence with everything I had. So how could I afford to be angry? I needed to get busy. I had a lot of work to do." Intense anger, fleeting depression and massive determination for action saved her life.

What to Do About It

- Move forward.
- Develop interests outside work.
- Build your self-esteem and sustain your sense of worth.

- Rediscover yourself. There are lots of other things you can do and now is the time to try.
- Turn your vision to the future in a positive way.
- Make a clean break with the past if necessary.

COMMON STRESSES
REBALANCING LIFE

Family, Work and Care-Giving

We assume that we are there to take care of our children until they gain a degree of independence. Why is the reverse such a problem? Care-giving at both ends of the life-span are stressful. Yet family relations and attitudes towards parents and grandparents put an added stress burden. Whereas in the past parents would be taken care of by someone in the family, they may now find they are fending for themselves or even being responsible for their own aging parents who are also living longer. Physical independence and health are concerns as friends start making the obituary columns. As boomers become seniors the added responsibility to care for two generations looms large. Why is this so surprising? As Beatrice Kirk, a friend's mother, observed, "A mother can take care of ten children, but ten children cannot seem able to care for one mother."

Today care-giving is a major source of stress for those caught in a delicate balancing act of work, family and care-giving. Unlike a growing child who is expected to be independent at some point in time, the task of a parent caregiver is of an unknown duration. Care-givers hold two and sometimes three full time jobs. They are frequently not only exhausted physically while actively caring, but emotionally and mentally drained, while worrying and anticipating around the clock. It is the classic case of stress burn-out.

So many women get caught up between family, job, caring for husband and children, and the needs of an aging parent. Giving care is the most noble of human compassions. It used to be that the nursing profession strictly had that responsibility since Florence Nightingale drew attention to this fact. But as the balance between able caregivers to those needing care is shifting, the social, personal, physical and financial impact of care giving needs to be addressed just as child care became accepted and recognized as a necessary social responsibility when working practices changed.

The cost of care is also huge. Added stress comes from the decision of how best to provide for a parent. Usually that caregiver is a daughter. Parents living with you entail a different kind of balancing act and safety considerations. Remaining in their own home which is what most prefer, either means family members carry the work load and emotional safety worries or find reliable visiting or in-home care to provide respite to the care-giver. Such in-home care comes with its own problems. You are not invincible. You are no good to the person receiving the care if you are no longer able to provide it. To avoid getting to this point, recruit the help of the care-receiver. Don't guess their needs. You are a team, both working towards the same end. Is something essential and must it be done right there and then at that very moment? For instance, agreeing with the care-receiver to go to a facility on weekends or for two to six weeks allows you to take a holiday, take a walk, a massage or a yoga class to breathe and relax.

Taking frequent time-outs will give you greater energy. You will feel better and provide better care. What do you do for yourself? Do not sacrifice the fundamentals of sleep, nutrition and movement. Get help. The same paid help or the same member of family can come at regular intervals, such as every Tuesday and Thursday afternoon, and allow you to plan appointments, errands, social activity or child care.

Recognize that it's a team effort. Care-giving is limited without the cooperation and motivation of the care-receiver. Before starting, sit down with your care-receiver. Honestly outline and discuss both your expectations. Recruit their participation. Seniors or spouses who have been used to being in charge and independent feel a loss of dignity when they find themselves on the receiving end. For others, if someone else makes the decisions, it allows them to complain. Explain the options available to each of you, their expectations and how working together and communicating openly will bring the best results.

Family or others responsible for the care are part of the team. Make sure to include them in the responsibility. This is a project. Plan it, treat it as such. Everyone needs to carry their weight. Unless you have an honest discussion with all concerned at the very start with frequent regular updates, not triggered by a crisis, you will end up carrying the entire load. Professional care-givers, nurses in Assisted Living Facilities, At Home Care or an ICU nurse experience the same pattern of physical and emotional burden as the family member.

Free or not, find out what helps others most and when and where you can get help when you need it. Have back-up systems. Use the professionals at the Employee Assistance Program at your workplace or talk to others who are in similar situations.

An example of non-coping seen frequently these days is 'caregivers' stress,' which especially afflicts the daughters of elderly parents who have Alzheimer's disease, dementia or have suffered a debilitating stroke. Because the image the caregivers carry in their heads from childhood is one of their parents taking care of them, they do not cope very well with the role reversal of them caring for their parents. Some do not cope at all. They do not dare leave their parents alone and are not willing to hand them over to other caregivers, so they go through social withdrawal hardly ever seeing anybody outside the immediate family.

Stress may also develop because of a neurotic need that may develop in the care-giver for control. Caregivers may become anxious, depressed, exhausted, and irritable. They act as if they own the problem. They need to learn coping skills, to relax and allow others to help and give them time off to recover. Making the care-giving a team process including sharing the responsibility with the care-receiver as well as other members of a family is the best solution for all. It is a matter of rebalancing responsibilities.

Caregiver's Burn-out

Anyone concerned or caring for another individual, temporary or chronic, is a candidate for burnout from too much stress. They could be caring for children, parents, a husband, partner or wife, a disabled child, friends, neighbors. Caring for others involves expending huge amounts of energy – physical, emotional, mental and spiritual. Eventually you will find yourself feeling completely overwhelmed.

When the needs of the care-receiver lead to personal neglect you may reach a point where you are no longer able to care effectively for the other person. Though we think of care-giving mainly in the sense of caring for a sick husband or parent, caring for a disabled child is also all-consuming. You may think that professional care-givers, nurses or doctors, would not have the emotional load that caring for a family member does, yet they frequently have a difficult time coming to terms, dissociating their emotions from their care-giving job.

Burn-out is the next step when you are giving out more than you take. You feel pulled in different directions. You may be criticized, not supported by family and friends. Even if appreciated, you can still feel drained.

Identify well before you need them individuals, organizations and resources for help.

What to Do About It

- Make structural changes to your home well before they are needed.
- Discuss frankly with all your family the wishes of the care-receiver and the sharing of care-giving responsibilities.
- Discuss with family honestly the sharing of work, family and care-giving balance.
- Recruit the help of the care-receiver.
- Get help to allow you time off

- Take frequent time-outs during the day
- Share the responsibility, costs and work with family
- Do not be a victim
- Plan it and treat it as a project
- Know your available resources.

Here is some excellent advice from Neil Lake's book *The Caregivers:*
- Try to do one thing at a time
- Be gently aware of loss or change
- Create good feelings with your care-receiver often
- Ask for help. Share your story
- Don't try to be a saint.

WHEN TO RETIRE

At 50 you are probably at the peak of your career. Enjoy it. This is no time to waste brooding about retirement.

Retirement has to do with work not life. It is about no longer doing a specific paying job. Don't let retirement be the end of life as well. On the contrary view it as the opportunity to do something you love passionately. If your work provided that passion, it is time for some introspection. Look around at the world and ask yourself what gives you most pleasure, that sense of fun.

There are two parts to this decision process: leaving a job and what will I do next? The word retirement has horrible connotations of being 'tired', suffering from fatigue and ready for the dump heap. In today's world this is far from true. Retirement age is an anachronism as well as wasting valuable talent and a much-needed public income-producing population. On the other hand, some people may indeed be ready to retire and should be encouraged to do so.

Gender Differences – Longevity

All over the world, women outlive men and many countries have far better life expectancy than in the US. For instance, women in Monaco have the world's longest lifespan, at 93.8 years, as do their men at 85.7 years. Danish women come a close second, with a life expectancy of 87.4. US women at 81.3 years lag way behind other countries while US men at 78.8 years rank 46th in life expectancy in the world.

Because men die younger, and a woman has usually taken care of her man, 70% of nursing home occupants in the US are women. Men are therefore much in demand in both nursing homes and retirement communities. Late in life partnerships are not at all uncommon.

What is the secret of women's greater longevity? If we could discover it could we use it to extend the lives of men? Women seem to have developed better stress-coping skills, not least through greater reliance on support groups. Under age 50, the social network of friends is made through their children at school and university, neighbors and dog-owners. Retirement especially if it involves moving may mean losing the social network both on the job as well as friends and associates made through work. Moving away may not be such a good idea.

In general, women are more socially interactive and are more communicative about their emotions than men. Managing stress and communicating with others appear to be aspects of life where women have an advantage. They are more likely to seek help, to make and keep friends, to be the care-givers of parents or grandchildren, and to volunteer to care for others.

Women are not only the more numerous among the elderly, they are also the poorer. Because most worked at lower paying jobs and their careers were often part-time or fragmented for family reasons, their pensions are lower than those of men. The need to work has been ever present whether single or married. However, women never retire completely because taking care of home and family is a lifetime job from which they can never retire. In essence, they never stop working, and in my opinion that is the secret of their longevity. They go downhill fast when they are put away in a retirement community or nursing care facility and no longer need to do the daily jobs, even though it may feel great for a little while.

On the other hand, men are more vulnerable to premature death. But once past the danger zone of 45 to 65, their life-expectancy increases, and the danger gap narrows. Men who live to 100 tend to have been self-employed and have rarely taken early retirement. In general, men over 90 function better mentally and physically than women of the same age probably because the male hormone testosterone does not drop as suddenly or as markedly in men as estrogen and testosterone do in women at menopause. Men also tend to have been and continue to be more physically active. More women suffer from dementia and Alzheimer's than men.

Men however, have the stress-edge over women when it comes to the challenge of modern technology. They seem less challenged by new appliances and gadgets, computers, cell phones, playing a DVD, recording a favorite program and other electronic devices. With a little patience and careful reading of the instructions, women generally catch up and discover the wonders of modern inventions. Computers, cell phones, burglar alarms, all remove the sense of isolation and helplessness that some may feel. Libraries nowadays provide wonderful services to teach you how to make the best use of such networking devices. An answer to almost any question can be found on Google!

What to Do About It

- Keep working it matters not at what.
- *Keep moving and playing.*
- Maintain a social network by weekly lunches with friends, a round of golf or serve on the committee of your local club, church or other organization.
- Learn something new; a language could take you to a local neighborhood to practice your Russian, juggling could be interesting to a school, volunteer time to tutor or take up cooking.

Keep on Working

If you miss working, then keep on working though it does not have to be at the same job. Working is good for your health. Economics apart, there are very good stress-fitness reasons for extending working life if you want to enjoy your later years to the full. Being paid for work is the most tangible evidence of worth, builds self-confidence, reinforces the sense of independence and provides positive feedback to your stress-controlling brain programs. For those who can afford it, volunteering also helps by being productive, maintaining social contacts and staying busy.

The vast majority of volunteers are women. Taking care of self, appearance, and feeling valued are major positive factors in remaining healthy and independent. Paid work is important to all. It is crucial for retired people to get dressed when they get up in the morning. Going somewhere, a walk, to shop, meet friends for coffee, the gym, a senior center, a book club are all cues and low-stress stimulation for the continuation of an active life.

The issue of when we should retire will continue to cause problems if it is only based on some arbitrary chronological age, for 'real age' is not the same for everybody. Suitable incentives should be provided for both employers and employees to motivate people to extend their working lives, albeit possibly not in the same job, nor at full pay.

Insurance companies could be encouraged to provide such incentives in the form of discounted premiums for people who remain earners longer. Just as the discounts for not smoking have contributed to saving many lives, premium reductions for staying lean and active would benefit both individuals and society.

On the financial front, couples do not always agree on when to retire. A husband might expect his working wife to retire when he does, when in fact she's not ready to quit her job. This is particularly so if he has the expectation that she would apply her full-time care and attention to his needs. What to do? Talk, talk, talk to each other. Couples often assume they both see retirement the same way but that is mostly untrue. The time to address and share what they expect to get out of retirement is before the decision is made about when to retire. At the same time if they have not shared information about their finances –and they should have – there is no excuse to put it off any further. It is no longer a question of whose job it is. Both stand to win or lose. Facing and discussing financial issues seem to be as personal, difficult and stressful as sex. The earlier in your relationship you begin to do this the better your relationship and your finances will be.

What to Do About It

- Do not base when you retire on age unless you have something ready to go into post retirement
- Talk, talk, talk. Do not make assumptions that others see your retirement as you do.
- Will the money last? Face and discuss your needs, budget and spending habits– the sooner the better.

Retirement Years

You can choose whether your retirement will be stressful or stress-free. As famous guitarist BB King said, "I never use that word retire." The traditional retirement gift is a watch or clock. It is kindly meant, but perhaps it also symbolizes a half-smothered thought that the recipient's real life is over, and all he or she can now do is count the days and wait to die. In fact, it is not unusual to hear stories of people who do die within a couple of years of retirement. They are the ones who have no passion, least of all a passion for life.

Travel may provide some temporary relief. I frankly cannot identify with the need to take one cruise after another. You may take a course but your heart is not in it. You have not engaged in sport for years except to watch it on TV. Your job was your life, and your friends were all work colleagues who within a year or so have become more distant. Your wife, after a short effort at trying to do things with you, goes back to her interests and friends.

Every time she goes to her exercise class or her bridge game you become more despondent. You bring down your toy train set from the attic but after the second day the magic is gone. So, you numb your helplessness with beer, pretzels, potato chips and TV or you sit in front of your computer. You forward reams of jokes to a list of people, most of whom you do not know. You play solitaire and surf the web looking for something that can give you an answer to your dilemma. To be brutally honest, you are waiting to die.

It seems to make no difference whether stopping work was mandatory or happened as the result of family pressure insisting that it was time for that well-earned rest! In my view, there will be plenty of time for rest once we are six feet under the ground, so why allow life to waste away now? Those who age successfully point to the importance of actively planning for retirement while including the pursuit of many interests and passions in the plan. This forward thinking is mostly started long before the dreaded date of parting from the structured life of daily office or factory.

Those lucky enough to work at an art, craft or science never really retire in the sense that they never stop thinking, learning, doing the job they love, though they may change the conditions under which they pursue it. Professional people, such as doctors or nurses, accountants or teachers, can turn to voluntary work. As a scientist, if I come across some new discovery I may despair that I do not understand the jargon. It is easy to give up and decide to retire my brain. Then I think of what I might be missing. So I turn to my young colleagues and ask them to explain. They love doing it and I may bring a different twist to their interpretations. They keep me up to date and they call me a walking encyclopedia – a win/win situation. I at last have the time to step back and look at my years of data and suddenly new interpretations pop up. Just as in writing this book research data and years of living came together in a productive way. I continue to learn from my readers. I am blessed.

Most people, however, used to the structure of many years of daily work do not know what to do with themselves in retirement. They become stressed-out. Despair and depression quickly sets in. The jobs around the house they had been able to avoid because of the excuse of work are an unavoidable burden. If pension or social security have removed the financial incentive for continuing to work, if your wife has her own social network, the children are now grown up and do not need you, and if all your life the job directed what you did, where now is your motivation to get up and do something?

What to Do About It

Life in retirement need not be like this.

- Focus on some pre-retirement career planning.
- Your finances may dictate when you retire. Analyze carefully when that might be.

- Face and discuss with your spouse how you envision retirement and the activities you would like to pursue.
- Consider you and your spouse's social network. If not developed the time to do so is before retirement.
- Take account of your health and financial status. The time to address each is before retirement.
- Be prepared instead of letting things happen.

Money

The biggest concern over money issues is whether there is enough and will the money last? Is your job in jeopardy? How much debt do you carry? Do you think about it when you use your credit card? How many credit cards do you own? Do you need more than one? There is always something suspicious about things that look 'easy'. Someone is getting rich out of your debt or your lack of vigilance. Are you in a position to carry all this debt? Are you reducing it or growing deeper in debt? The answers to these questions depend on each one of us. It's time to relieve your stress. Lifestyle will change.

Some expenses such as transportation will diminish as the daily commute is no longer necessary. The type of clothes you wear may change and the office wardrobe, dry cleaning and shoe costs will lessen. On the other hand, other expenses may increase such as fitness activities, travel, and staying electronically connected, perhaps once covered by the employer, will now have to come from your own pocket. It is a balancing act.

It is crucial at this major junction in your life to selfishly take a good hard look at your budget, needs and spending habits. Your budget must be reorganized to address your new lifestyle. This is the time to set priorities and pay attention to what is essential rather than paying for something you rarely use. Perhaps you need to wean some relatives from the gifts they had become used to receiving from you. They have grown up. You can change the type of gift you give; it's the thought that counts.

There is no need to add to your stress level with matters you can easily control. Being prepared instead of letting things happen can make all the difference to your continued financial peace of mind.

On the other hand, you have no way of knowing how long you will live and whether your savings will see you through. Most retired persons I know relied on an acceptable interest rate on their investments for their gift giving, their annual trip and their little splurges like eating out with friends. The recession of the last ten years saw interest rates collapse to nothing, severely denting their sense of independence. They may come back but in the meantime costs will rise and you will be older.

As long as you don't go on too many wild spending sprees, why worry? A colleague used to say that he wanted to die broke. That is equally impossible to gauge. The best solution is to enjoy living, be grateful to work as long as you can, and make sure you continue the habit of saving even a small amount for the little extras in life or for a fun investment. If you have saved and made sensible investments all your life there is every reason for your money to see you through.

Money is not everything, but the quality of life that so much depends on the state of your health and your capacity to enjoy the later years can also depend on the size of your wallet. The current trend of people living longer and the likelihood that life-spans will increase even further over the next 50 years have generated alarm among economists and politicians. How can the population still at work support and provide medical care for this mushrooming segment of pensioners? In 2021, the first of the USA's 76 million baby boomers will turn 75.

I have met women in their 70s whose husband dies. He always took care of their finances because he claimed it "was a man's job." Now what? She has no idea where she stands financially, where the records are. Did they have joint accounts? Who are the beneficiaries? Who can she turn to that she can trust and who has no claim on her finances. To top it all, she often cannot even drive. Stories of older women who are swindled by clever con-men abound. Don't be one of them. Do not be forthcoming with information about your social security number and personal data on accounts. *Not only is work good for your health but it is good for the country.*

What to Do About it

- Be prepared instead of letting things happen
- Selfishly take a good hard look at your budget, needs and spending habits.
- Before you go on a spending spree recognize that you are assuming costs your employer used to pay.
- Are your medical care costs covered?
- There is no harm in cutting back on gifts.
- Continue the habit of saving.

- If you cannot drive, now is the time to learn.
- Begin with your last income tax file. You signed it? Now read it. It should have all the information you need. Talk to your accountant or find a new one. Ask questions. Get on top of things.
- Check with your library they may be able to recommend someone.
- Make a budget, assess what you have, know where the money goes, where it comes from and where you stand at any moment.
- There you are. By just being knowledgeable and prepared you have significantly cut your stress level.
- Thinking of downsizing? Do it before you retire. Find a home on one floor with ramps for some future time when you might need them. Going up and down steps is good for your health as long as you have the option of not having to use them. A smaller, cheaper-to-maintain, less-work home with fewer outgoings, property taxes or association dues, could give you peace of mind and money in your pocket.
- There is evidence that people who continue to work and enjoy it, remain healthy longer. As in my case, retirement from one career does not mean you will no longer work but you will have the freedom to choose perhaps something different or follow your passion. Studies have shown that in order to remain healthy, you should keep on working, preferably at something you like or with people you like — not merely as a volunteer.

HEALTH ISSUES LOOM LARGER

Did you get into bad eating habits? Do you grab ready- to-heat food, prepared and preserved because it is easier to handle? Or is the pizza delivery boy a regular feature every evening at your door? Does your body's reflection in the mirror remind you of a changing shape? Have you kept up your exercise or other activity habits or are you so tired at the end of a day that you slump in a chair to watch TV? Do you get good and adequate sleep? Has your bed-time changed over the first 50 years? Do you fall asleep on the couch or even in bed with the TV on or the lights on while reading? Did you get into the habit of taking a sleeping pill? Do you wake up groggy with aches and pains?

Or maybe you have had a more serious illness – diabetes, heart issues or high blood pressure, asthma or arthritis, perhaps an encounter with breast cancer? Do you have acid reflux or other gut problems that give you pain and make you miserable? Are you depressed and need medication?

What do you do to feel better? Maybe more than one glass of wine or some sort of pill might help? You cannot stop smoking, or maybe you have not shed your social drug habit.

The Health – Stress Relationship

Stress causes or aggravates a variety of health problems from diabetes, heart conditions to cancer. On the other hand, how healthy you are and your lifestyle habits determine how well you respond to stress. We all know that the healthier we are, the better we survive the flu season without getting sick. It also follows that you will have fewer medical care costs. Or you may worry about aches and pains that begin to creep up on you. Arthritic hands, back-pain and tight jaw-line from grinding your teeth at night all get worse with stress.

You may already have health issues. Disorders that used to be considered those of old age are now seen at an ever younger age even in children. If you escaped them before, this is when they will appear. High blood pressure, a heart attack or stroke, diabetes, breast, prostate, colon and other cancers, and loss of memory or depression are possible. More and younger people are developing dementia and other brain-related diseases than ever before.

A large British study compared the health and mortality rates of people 55-74 year olds from 1979-81 and 2008-10 from highly technologically developed countries such as the US, Canada, Britain, Germany, and Japan. The results showed a shocking spike in the number of deaths from neurological diseases such as dementia and Alzheimer's in 2010 – more in women than men and too rapid to be due to any mass genetic change. Professor Pritchard (2013), the lead author, attributes the rapidity of these changes to environmental, and societal changes "increased population, economic activity, air and road traffic and more home technology including background electromagnetic fields, mobile phones, microwave ovens, computers, which are unique to the last 30 years."

These are all novel, modern-day stresses. What could have happened to our brain in such a short period that would have made it so vulnerable to damage? Probably all of these factors contribute and particularly a change in lifestyle that weakens our defenses across the board. Modern technologies operate

24/7 giving the brain no respite or time-out and therefore no chance of recovery.

Poor or inadequate sleep, eating and drinking habits, how many hours you sit each day in front of a computer, the TV or in a car or office or even playing bridge, all contribute to your general state of health.

Poor Sleep seems to be a trade mark of those crossing the 50+ line. Sleep deprivation — deprivation of REM sleep, that portion of sleep when dreaming occurs — and cumulative sleep loss have all been found to affect the response to stress. Half of US adults are sleep deprived reports the Center for Disease Control. The majority of Americans, 63%, don't get the eight hours of sleep recommended by experts for good health. The American Psychological Association reports that the 50+ workers in particular get fewer than six to six and a half hours sleep a night – significantly less than the recommended minimum. This is not good for their cognitive skills, memory, moral judgment, reaction time, irritability, creativity, immune system, risk of heart disease and stroke, aches and pain, affecting their overall health.

STRESS –> POOR SLEEP –> MORE STRESS

It is a vicious cycle. Stress keeps you awake. Less sleep or poorer quality of sleep prime your body to overreact to stress. You are awakened to empty your bladder and cannot go back to sleep. Worries about things you can do nothing about – the '*what if*' stresses – flood your brain. You cannot go back to sleep. You reach for a sleeping pill. You wake up groggy. You get depressed.

Sleep physiologist David Dinges at the University of Pennsylvania showed that not only was health affected, but the cumulative reduction over a period of days of an amount of sleep as short as 20 minutes per day increased fatigue, errors in work-related activities, confusion and decreased concentration. Sleep-deprived individuals are more susceptible to stress, mood changes and emotional issues and are prone to road accidents.

Sleep habits that change with age may not only affect how much sleep you get but its quality as well. Older adults still need seven to eight hours of sleep per night. Complaints of difficulty falling or staying asleep are more common as is the incidence of sleep apnea leading to feeling less refreshed on awakening in the morning. Sleeping pill use is greater in older adults as well. If you recognize any of these symptoms please ask your doctor to be tested for sleep apnea. It keeps you awake and you reach for your sleeping pill. Sleep apnea means you are breathing in *less oxygen*. Your brain becomes deprived of oxygen and gets sluggish. It interferes with a good night's sleep, as does the turned on TV screen in your bedroom or the lights on the digital clock or even your reading tablet. These inhibit the hormone melatonin which helps you sleep. Sleeping pills or a glass of wine late at night are not the solution.

Cumulative sleep loss – a total of less than 7 hours a night, even without apnea, leads to a greater stress response. Your cognitive skills are affected. Memory loss, impaired moral judgment, decreased creativity, symptoms similar to ADHD (Attention Deficit Hyperactive Disorder), jumpiness, slower reaction time, decreased accuracy, tremors, aches, increased heart variability, risk of heart disease and stroke, an impaired immune system and sleepiness during the day have all been documented. Missing sleep certainly affects the way you feel and function. These consequences are not only bad for your health, but they can also seriously impact your career, driving and family life.

What to Do About It

- Set the scene for good sleep. Try not to eat or drink anything for at least three hours before going to bed.
- Do not take phone calls for an hour before sleep.
- Turn down the lights in your sitting room
- Make sure your bedroom is dark at night – no digital clocks, phones recharging, TV or other turned-on electronic devices.
- Reading light only one that focuses on the book not your eyes.
- If you get up at night do not turn on the lights. Use a small night-light only in the bathroom.
- Try to get 7-8 hours of sleep lying in bed per night.
- Be active during the day.
- Ask your doctor to be tested for sleep apnea or restless leg syndrome. If you snore chances are you are not getting enough oxygen while you sleep.

Moving Less as while moving spontaneously about your house or garden all day, is a crucial part of our daylight hours. Too much sitting, in itself a stress, is now known to be an independent risk factor for cancer, diabetes, stroke and heart conditions and balance and coordination problems. New appliances and technologies encourage you to move less. Hours of continuous sitting in front of the computer or TV, taking the elevator, driving a car or riding a bus or train have replaced spontaneous movement. Even exercise once a day does not counteract the effects of such prolonged sitting.

MOVE LESS– MORE STRESS

It's a vicious cycle. The fact that we move less than we used to and move even less in our later years, makes us even less able to move at all. Uninterrupted sitting is a stress in itself. We lose our balance and coordination. We are afraid of falling. Coupled with the loss of bone mass, the thought of breaking a hip or a wrist fills us with horror. In most cases, that is a one-way street to the nursing home.

On the other hand, being active and exercising relaxes you, helps you sleep and better digest what you eat. Moving about increases the circulation of blood, oxygen and glucose carried to the brain making you calmer, better prepared to face daily stresses. Exercise alone does not counteract the effects of sitting all day. If you cannot or do not have time or energy to exercise make sure you are as active as you possibly can be inside the house or garden. It will help you remain independent as long as you live.

What to Do About It

- Make a point of standing up often – every 20 or 30 minutes.
- If watching TV stand up during commercials.

- Go up and down stairs at every opportunity.
- A daily walk is good but being active all day as well is even better.
- Exercise when you can but that is not as good as moving about all day.
- Test yourself. Rise from your chair without leaning on anything.
- Take a Yoga class.
- Walk instead of driving if you can.
- Avoid the elevator and escalator.
- Work in the garden. Enjoy the sun.

Overdoing Exercise can be just as bad as not moving enough. In your search for youth and vigor is your paunchy shape and loss of fitness or the stress in your life driving you to overtrain? Perhaps training to run a local marathon may keep you motivated. Though exercise is good for your health, with benefits to your immunity and cardiovascular system, training for a Marathon requires that you start out with a certain level of fitness. Overtraining can be deadly. The first London Marathon in 1981 was the brain child of Chris Brasher who won gold in the 3,000 meter steeplechase in the 1956 Olympics in Melbourne. Over the last 50 years and hot on the heels of the fitness and aerobic craze, of the late 70s and 80s, almost every large city in the world now organizes an annual Marathon. Fueled by the media, raising money for a charity or any number of other reasons they have become popular and lucrative for the city and fun for the participants. But excessive physical stress from overtraining is itself a stress and can lead to respiratory infections. As for any stress making sure you adequately recover between workouts is the simplest solution to avoiding damage. Dietary supplements like *nutritional yeast* (not brewer's yeast) a food rich in magnesium and B vitamins, may help you recover faster. Overtraining can lead to adrenal fatigue which is also seen when your are burned out from excess physical or mental stress.

What to Do About It

- As you approach 50 and have been inactive do not jump into training for a Marathon.
- Become aware of your physical and mental stress.
- Ease into a daily exercise routine gently to improve your fitness.
- Avoid overtraining
- Take nutritional yeast to help you recover faster from overtraining
- Reduce the hours you sit by being more active all day.
- Are your eating habits healthy?
- Get adequate sleep.
- Learn breathing exercises to help you relax

Eating Right is another key factor that affects how you respond to stress. Almost every prepared food these days is loaded with pesticides, weed killers and fertilizers used to grow fruits and vegetables. Extra hormones are fed to animals to tenderize and 'beef up' other meats. Most fish and eggs are contaminated. Even the packaging or the ways fruit and vegetables are packaged to prevent them from tuning brown or going bad, or even bread from drying is done with chemicals. There is a reason the baguette in France goes hard and dry in one day and ours lasts, or sliced bread seems to last forever without going moldy. Since throwing away moldy bread was a sin at home, my father resorted to persuading me that I would turn blond if I ate it!

SUGARS, TOXIC CONTAMINANTS AND ADDITIVES = MORE STRESS

Eating sugar is a stress. Foods are processed and preserved with additives to extend their shelf-life. They are by-products of the oil industry and are toxic chemicals. Introduced into your body in food they are perceived as a threat. A stress defense reaction for survival is initiated to defend you. Your body cannot get rid of all these toxins.

Read labels. If you see words you do not recognize chances are they are synthetic additives. Avoid anything that sounds like a chemical, food loaded with preservatives, fortified with well-meaning vitamins and minerals, a GMO food. You are paying with your health for the chemicals that humans have discovered to keeping food seem fresh, colorful and last longer. If you ate fresh food you would not need to have it fortified.

Drinking fluoride-free water and staying well-hydrated is good for your brain which is where your stress is processed and the response initiated. Sugar in large quantities is toxic and certainly should be kept low if you have a tendency towards diabetes or obesity. More sugar is added to increase the weight of cereal or a chocolate bar. Sodium is added as salt to soda pop to make you thirsty so that you drink more. Then sugar is added to cover up the saltiness. Avoid anything that is described as 'free' of fat or sugar. What is taken out of the food is often replaced with a synthetic something that is even less healthy than the fat or sugar that was taken out in the first place.

Reduce or eliminate sugar of any kind from your diet including honey. You get plenty of sugar from the fruits you eat, and even that should be limited. Avoid dairy foods. Milk contains lactose, a sugar. On the other hand, butter which is only the fat from the milk is much healthier. It certainly is healthier than trans-fats.

Those of us who are in the older brackets of the over-50s are luckier in not having been exposed as much to these preservatives, toxins and hormone-fed animals of today as we were growing up. It may be one reason we live longer.

There are many simple ways you can improve your diet to better your health. Sleeping and eating are interdependent. Recent work has shown that sleep deprivation increases eating. Eating leads to storing most of that energy as fat. Stressed women are more likely to crave sugar; they have a larger hip circumference and more belly fat (Mocedo & Diez, 2014).

The foods we eat create small injuries compounding bigger injuries causing the body to respond continuously to inflammation. The more we consume prepared and processed food, the more we trip the inflammation switch little by little each day.

What to Do About It

- Choose whole foods your grandmother served and not those manufactured foods filling the grocery store aisle.

- Avoid sugars including honey and fructose.
- Eat more fruits and vegetables.
- Choose organic or, even better, grow your own. You can then control your exposure to highly toxic pesticides, weed killer and fertilizer.
- Eat more fish preferably from a wild source, and oily to be rich in omega-3 fatty acids
- Avoid dairy. Milk contains lactose, a sugar.
- Read labels.
- Get a good night's sleep and be active all day.
- Grow your own vegetables to control for pesticides and fertilizers.

LOSS AND GRIEVING

We mostly think of loss as something that older persons have to deal with. That is so if we strictly think of loss in terms of family and friends who have died. After the initial shock of losing someone, we experience the *void* the loss a person has left. The death of a child at any age is doubtless the most severe loss we can experience. Not only are we deprived of our flesh and blood, but also of the emotional aspirations we have built up for the yet unlived future of that child.

We grieve for ourselves – for the impact the loss of someone or something will have on us. Yes, it sounds selfish and unkind but that's what it boils down to. Helplessness often follows the loss of a husband. A wife has been used to be cared for, driven and the finances taken care of by her spouse. She refuses to drive and panics over writing a check. Expecting friends and relatives to step in to fill the void is unfair and irrational, willing as friends might be. It is time to step up to the challenges. Services provided by communities and churches can help. It is not enough for a husband to leave his wife well taken care of if he did everything for her. It is the spouse's responsibility to make sure she or he is capable of taking care of everything after one is gone; find things, who to trust and what to expect.

The top eight stressful Life Events one thinks of that deal with loss may not appear to be serious losses at first glance. Being jailed or married deal with loss of freedom? Who has not experienced stress at misplacing keys, glasses, the loss of hair or a wallet? Trivial as that may seem compared to losing a friend, a job, a home or lost health or independence, the stages of grieving that one goes through are the same. It is the amount of time you dwell in each stage that varies depending on your resilience. Different people dwell longer at the different stages of this scheme.

Elizabeth Kuebler Ross, a Swiss psychiatrist, described these stages as *Denial, Anger, Bargaining, Depression* and *Acceptance (DABDA)*.

Denial is a natural first reaction. "I don't believe it" no matter what the "it" refers to. Don't hide your pain. Denial makes healing take longer.

Anger at how something like this could happen to you. Someone else must be to blame. Anger and fear are destructive, all-consuming and can lead to violence. Placing the blame on others or one's own guilt fuels the flames of anger. What did I do wrong? His children did not care about him just his money. Grudges and revenge within and between families and countries fill books of history. To move on you must learn to let go and forgive.

Bargaining is the negotiating stage whether with your doctor, lawyer, husband, or some greater power, to reverse events.

Depression follows when reality sinks in. More people seem to be suffering from depression these days and resort to medication. Most often it is due to loneliness, as a result of the loss of social contact or support. Seeking fellowship in friends and family is the answer to loneliness. Web-based social networking is not quite as rewarding. Go where you may find people who put their hand out and touch you. Notice the signs of depression and seek help for them. Be grateful for what you do have. Whatever your problem there are others somewhere who are worse off. Reach out and help them. You will feel better.

Anger requires active letting go and forgiving to get over it. Similarly, *Depression* requires serious introspection to address the person's relationship to the loss. Expert guided help is useful in moving through these steps smoothly into a new relationship with the person lost.

Acceptance, the final stage, is not resignation but rather an active stage of resuming and appreciating life. You do not forget someone or get over a loss. You adapt and move forward. You restructure your life, learning from the experience making your journey through the loss part of the new you. Give yourself time over the loss. You do not and must not forget. Healing takes time. Remembering is useful in growing with the process of healing until you come to a new steady state with the memory of the person or item lost. It has been a setback. Find someone who has survived a similar loss – a spouse, a home, a job, a child.

LOSS, DEPRESSION AND ACCEPTANCE

At a talk I gave at the Stanford Health Library a sad older couple sat in the front row. I asked people to share their stresses and finally they spoke up. They had lost a son to leukemia. Loss of a child may be the worst loss to go through. I asked about when the son had died. "Eleven years ago" came the answer. Turns out they had been stuck in the *Depression* stage for all that time and had not moved on to the final stage of *Acceptance*. They faced their loss as a setback. Nothing had been moved in their home since he died; neither had they moved on but were immobilized, brooding.

You will not be able to feel the touch or hug of someone physically. Integrate their presence virtually into your life with positive and humorous experiences. What would they have thought or said leads to positive integration of the lost one into your daily living. It takes time. Don't rush it.

GRIEF

"The reality is that you will grieve forever. You will not 'get over' the loss of a loved one; you will learn to live with it. You will heal and you will rebuild yourself around the loss you have suffered. You will be whole again but, you will never be the same. Nor should you be the same, nor would you want to."
—Elizabeth Kuebler-Ross and John Kessler

What to Do About It

- Recognize loss as a normal every day reaction that causes you stress.

- Recognize that you are grieving the loss as it affects *you* and that therefore it is in your power to modify that reaction or at least its intensity.
- Ask yourself 'what is the worst thing that could happen to you as a result of this loss?'
- Become aware of the processing steps you take in all cases of loss.
- Become aware of the stages of loss. Where you are at the present moment?
- Seek help from friends or social support to communicate your feelings.
- Do not get stuck in *Anger* or *Depression*.
- Take the time you need to go through the stages.

Loneliness

Loneliness is one form of reacting to loss. It may be incidental or deliberate withdrawal. Family can be a great source of joy or an enormous stress even if often unknowingly. Having grown up in families where the parents and grandparents lived alone or with the family, it pains me to see how many persons relegated to a nursing home are rarely visited. Only persons who had absolutely no one left in the world were taken in by nursing homes. Those who lived alone used to be called every day by children or a family member.

In the age of 24-hour-a-day fingertip access to a telephone, it is no longer a question of access or time to call. It is not enough to remember parents on Mother's Day. Do we love our parents any less today? Probably not. We simply do not value them and hence care about them as much. Maybe since they took care of us and balanced home and work life so well we have not realized that they now need our care in return; but beware of treating them as a child. Are they hard to get along with? Are we overwhelmed by their undivided parental attention? That only means we have not outgrown childhood sufficiently to be able to get the best out of our parents by smiling away the paternal or maternal reflex actions. Our materialistic culture has made us so self-centered, money- and thing-oriented that we believe we have fulfilled our responsibilities when we turn over care to a third party by buying the service.

What we do not realize is how much stress we are causing and what we are missing by doing that. Apart from inflicting the pain of isolation and loneliness, we are depriving ourselves of huge stress-relief benefits. We go looking for someone else to talk to. We may even pay a professional for this service when we have it there all along. And that all-important hug to relieve stress? No one is better at hugging than a mother.

What to Do About It

- Make the effort to stay in touch with family and friends.
- Reach out and touch somebody. You will get much benefit.
- Make that unexpected call or write a proper letter.
- Nurture your circle of friends. They will be there when you need them.

Family – Stress or Solution

There is no family that does not have a problem. Looking back to your first 50 years you have come across your own problems

– a child who needs special care, a rebellious teen-ager; alone or married both come with their own issues; your parents went through a divorce and you felt abandoned; you were abused and cannot forgive and let go.

Children leave home, you feel loss but soon realize they never really leave. First, they need their laundry done. They come home for a good meal. They get upset if you clear out and redecorate their bedroom. They have the same expectations of you throughout life. They need you. They may change but you are not supposed to. You never retire from the parenting job.

An important twist in the parent child relationship progresses as you age. You never cease or become unable to offer advice. But do you listen to them and how do you get the younger generation to listen to you as you get older. Your experience, your Data Base may be different but events and emotions repeat themselves. There is much wisdom to convey. Equally and more significantly how do you get them to listen to you. How can the youngest generation faced with added layer of older generation benefit as well as become aware of the needs of elders? It is no surprise that grandchildren seem to pay more attention and have a better relationship with elders than their own children.

Now past 50, empty-nesters have to readjust to living with each other again. If parents divorce, or separate, children may sever relations with one of them. As you get older it gets particularly stressful to be out of contact with your children and grandchildren and a big loss to them even though they may not appreciate it till it might be too late.

Illness and loss may hit someone in the family. Even if you keep yourself healthy, they may not. They will turn to you for help. At 50+ you get caught up in any family feud. You are judged even if you try to be even-handed. Unless you address the stress of taking sides head-on, you may carry this burden throughout your life. It makes you sick. No amount of doctors and pills can fix your pain.

What to Do About It

- Learn to let go. Call it forgive or whatever it is. Do not carry a grudge or guilt.
- Do not take sides in family feuds.
- Stay in touch with family. They are the only one you have.
- Take the first step to reconcile.
- Keep your relationship within whatever limits you wish. Do not allow family to take over your life. Say No sometimes if warranted.
- Put aside the parent/child, old/young lifetime presumptions and get in the habit of truly listening to each other's needs as well as advice. Make a special event of it.

AGE CHALLENGE AND BENEFITS

Are the stresses after age 50 any different from what younger persons experience? There are a lot more people over 50 because many are living longer, more active lives into their 70s, 80s and even 90s. In particular, as baby-boomers are entering the ranks of seniors they see retirement and old age as two different phases. The six most likely events that come with getting older — retirement, loss of a significant other, a possible change in finances and standard of living, care-giving of an older parent, relocation when it is our turn to receive care and how we face our life's end.

An important Harris poll conducted in 2009 on behalf of Charles Schwab's *OnInvesting* magazine found that most people today no longer see this period in their lives as a time to "wind down, but rather as a new phase of life with exciting new opportunities." They see "retirement and old age as two completely different things." Retirement is associated with when Social Security kicks in, old age as beginning at 85. This is not quite what your granddaughter or grandson would define as "old."

On our 50th birthday we suddenly become aware of our mortality though the odds are good that we will have another 30 or even 50 years to live. What's the point of wasting them brooding? As the antiques dealer said, "the older my wife gets, the more I appreciate her."

Yet the stress challenges that face us typically do change with age. The ability to keep some sense of personal control is eroded by other peoples' attitudes and preconceptions about age, as well as by our own physical slowing down. Both of these can be corrected. Getting a senior discount card at a restaurant is good. So is the "I did not think you were that old!" look from the cashier. But something as minor as the need for reading glasses can be a major blow to one's vanity and independence. It can affect the ability to drive, for one thing. Cataract surgery can come to the rescue by becoming a relatively simple procedure these days. Waning sex, love, physical strength and memory are all stress candidates. But there is much that can be done to bring these worrisome stressors under control. After all, the outcome is to a huge extent in the eyes of the beholder. Generations that grew up with the saving ethos and found it difficult to owe money to anyone, now worry about whether the money will last.

On the other hand we mellow. There are advantages that come with the accumulated experience of passing years. What is taken for wisdom is the result of acquired competence, patience and being less judgmental. We hold fewer grudges, less anger or disgust. We tend to whine less, well, some of us. We still get grumpy and irritated but it does not last as long. We are more affectionate, compassionate and definitely see the funny side of almost everything. We are more forgiving and generous to a fault. We make great grandparents because whether we can hear or not we have time to listen and appear to understand.

Have you noticed how once you cross over 50 you seem to get along better with younger persons? Skipping one or two generations seems to make all the difference. They want to know about us and our experiences and we can, in turn, enjoy listening to their view of life.

What to Do About It

- Do whatever needs doing to remain healthy and independent as long as you live.
- Have cataract or macular degeneration surgery for failing vision

- Get a hearing aid for failing hearing.
- Be active.
- Take care of your physical appearance. There is always plastic surgery if desperate. Maintain your appearance and personal health.
- Keep up your balance and good posture whether you sit or move about.
- To keep going as you age, persuade yourself and others of your usefulness. Pursue something passionately. Keep working and associate with younger people. You have so much to contribute, write it down, share it, make them aware of it.
- Let them know you are not going anywhere real fast.

Care-Receiving

Will you need someone to care for you? How will you feel as the care–receiver? Are you not stressed? Staying healthy and independent means that increasing responsibilities become harder to control. This includes managing every day self-care, washing, eating cooking, making one's own choices and delaying or minimizing total dependence on others. Making structural changes to your home will help you maneuver, remain mobile as long as possible.

Time comes when we can no longer drive safely. It is not just the eyes, it is also upper body rotation and reflexes With this comes loss of independence. We feel that we have become a burden. Feelings of loneliness and helplessness are highly stressful. We no longer feel useful to our family. We were the ones who cared for them and now the tables are turned. We become angry at ourselves for our increasing helplessness and find it hard to accept help. We become demanding. We are going through our own stress of loss of independence. We end up making it harder on the giver. Nursing home or assisted living looms ahead. If we feel we are treated like a child, speaking up and having a frank discussion with our care-giver is far better than anger.

It is best if all affected parties are logically involved in the decision and choice. Self-sacrifice by the care-giver is not the answer either. It is best if we remain aware and actively take responsibility for maintaining our health and mobility as long as possible. Care-giver and care-receiver are in a compassion-gratitude bond that could be a win-win situation.

These days Wellness Centers have sprung up everywhere and provide classes and training for all ages. Transportation is also provided by most communities. There is always something we can do to be helpful.

My aunt Calypso recently died at 105 years old. She lived with her daughter and son-in-law; had her own room and little garden. Her room was impeccably clean and tidy. She could get around with a walker for safety. Her only complaint was poorer vision which prevented her from sewing. However, she had always enjoyed housework and had for years made it her job to polish the silver. And when she was through she started again! It had been a source of pride and accomplishment. Her other job was to water the houseplants. Occasionally they may have gotten a double dose but the plants didn't seem to mind. There was always something to do that others would rather not.

Relocation, in particular to a nursing home, is invariably a one-way street. Psychologist Judy Rodin, former President of the University of Pennsylvania, did some important research when teaching coping skills to the residents of a nursing home. She worked with them and the staff to reduce the tendency of elderly people to attribute their shortcomings to their physical state. For example, they were told that the floors of the nursing home were very slippery because they were tiled to keep them clean. Even young people could slip on them. In this way the residents would refocus their own thinking and stop blaming weak knees or poor coordination, passing the stress of the blame instead to a realistic factor in the environment. Residents in nursing homes often have very high cortisol stress levels, similar to those found in patients suffering from depression. Acquiring coping skills and learning how to perceive having greater control of their lives reduced their cortisol levels to normal and improved their general well-being.

Even more than being taken care of, it is most important to be needed, whether visited, or asked to do something useful.

What to Do About It

As the **care-receiver** make your needs known realistically. Identify ways that you can participate in your own care-receiving journey.

- As the care-receiver do everything in your power to remain as healthy and active as possible as long as you live.
- Make structural changes to your environment well before they are needed
- Discuss frankly with all your family your wishes about your care.

- Remain involved in any decisions about living and caring adjustments your family is considering and the financial considerations.
- Participate in identifying resources for help. Don't let things happen.

Independence

Take away independence and you lose your individuality; you generate stress. My late friend Tom Rogers frequently said, "I want to be healthy till I drop dead." That statement hides the most powerful desire in all of us. We all want to remain independent — to be able to stand up and move about, be healthy enough to drive a car and continue to live at home for the rest of our life. No one wants the stress of feeling a burden to others. Nor do we find the prospect of being well looked-after in a nursing home a quality of life to aspire to. Independence means freedom to choose — when and what to eat, when to sleep and wake up, whom to see, talk to or what to do.

Can independence be retained, and if so how? If you give up, if you retire from life, your body and brain will give up on you. Independent seniors share common attitudes. They continue to have a passion for life and people around them; curiosity and taking on new challenges are characteristic. It can be as simple as getting out of their chair unaided, to learning how to play bridge or the guitar. Look at Tony Bennett holding his own at 88 on stage with Lady Gaga at 28! Does he need the money? Hardly. He does need the emotional reward, the joy of living and working with others of all ages.

Examples abound of physical achievements in sports. Sport gives a sense of accomplishment and control thereby overcoming stress-out. More and more elderly people walk in shopping malls or work out in the gym. There are special classes for those once thought too delicate and frail to exercise. It is no longer rare to see runners, cyclists and, of course, golfers riding their carts, well into their seventies.

John Glenn, 94 in 2015, after returning to space at 77 in 1998, was campaigning for President Obama at 87 years old in 2008. Ann Boyle Gallagher of Alexandria, Virginia skydived for the first time at 78. Asked why, she said it was on her list of things to do. These people do not have time to be stressed nor to be old.

Markets are changing to meet this new sports sector. The Senior Olympics in the US and the European Veterans' Athletics Championships provide grueling competition. The United States Tennis Association now has an over-90s tennis league. What keeps such people going? The late Dodo Cheney said at 90: "Competition; keep doing it; play through your injuries; don't stop".

There are many ways one can keep busy and make extra cash too. There is always need for a reliable driver for runs to airports, errands or doctors' appointments. A special license may be required. Median pay could be $15/hour plus cost of gas if you are using your car. If you are good with languages you could be a translator or interpreter. Spanish, Mandarin, Arabic and Korean in addition to the European languages are needed for translating in court as well as in the work environment. You could earn from $11 to $40 hourly. I love seeing those helpful employees of a certain age at Lowe's.

Good for all of them. Or if you like fixing things why not put your skills to good use. Pay starts at around $15 and goes up to $40 per hour.

Big demand will increasingly exist for caregiver relief as more and more working people will need someone to take over being with their loved one for a few hours – parent-sitting, not unlike house-sitting, pet-sitting, or baby-sitting. Just as the need for organized child-care has evolved in the last 50 years, so will parent-care-giving. For some reason churches have not stepped up to this need. This is the time to get creative.

What to Do About It

- Go visit a nursing home. It is enough to get you moving.
- Make it your goal to get up and sit down on a toilet seat without leaning on anything. Even better try squatting as needed for some toilets.
- Move about all day in the home, garden, up and down stairs, laugh, houseclean, dance and do a sport if you can.
- Eat sensibly by reading labels.
- Get lots of good sleep by following earlier guidance.
- Hang on to your drivers' license by staying healthy.
- Be good to your friends.

End of Life

No one believes or thinks about dying any time soon, certainly not in our 20s or 30s. We have too much living to do. Yet as we cross the 50+ line we become aware of the finish line creeping closer. Are we filled with terror or just put it out of our mind? Have we come to terms with the finite nature of life that sooner or later it will be our turn? As daily Obituaries of friends and acquaintances remind us we are not immortal.

Each one of us has to face it alone. We can seek information from our church or compare the attitudes to death of various religions. For first hand information visit a Hospice, volunteer to work there or speak with Hospice workers. Then draw your own conclusions.

JANE FONDA INTERVIEWED BY AARP AT 78
She makes it a point of "cozying up to death and making it a friend. That's what I always do with things that frighten me…. It helps me to plan. If you know you want to have certain loved ones around you, then you have to live in ways that you will have them there. And you don't want important things going unsaid before you die. Death is inevitable. So why not make peace with it?"

What to Do About It

- Talk about it with your close friends. What are their thoughts on the subject?
- Discuss it with your family if you can
- If you have not done so, make a will, and a living Trust?
- Document your assets annually
- Update your filing so others can find documents
- After consulting with your family as to their preferences, mark with colored stickers items that are to go to various members.

- Make arrangements of how you would like others to handle your end of life and burial.
- Join a group that might discuss the subject.
- If you cannot care for yourself, how would you like to be cared for?
- Discuss it with your family.
- Visit a hospice to find out how others have handled this situation.
- Explore how different religions and communities address this issue and join a discussion group.
- Make it simple for those around you.

ATTITUDE

Looking forward instead of dwelling in the past is essential to a positive attitude and a great way to dismiss most nagging stress. Enjoy the moment. If you do not find something to look forward to, you will soon have a hard time getting out of bed in the morning. In far too many nursing homes, the residents find that yesterday, today and tomorrow all blur into the same monotonous repetitive routine while mindlessly watching some talking head on the TV screen. The staff, however well-meaning, does not help if it treats the residents like patients or children.

When I first started running studies with healthy young volunteers who remained continuously in bed for seven days, I noticed that they soon started behaving like patients in a hospital. The staff, used to caring for the sick lying in bed, treated them as such. If asked how they felt, the volunteers eagerly listed all their childhood illnesses — chicken pox, measles, and all. This was hardly the way to foster a positive attitude, so we quickly put a stop by removing trappings and behaviors associated with hospitals. White lab-coats were replaced by colorful aprons. Staff no longer wore stethoscopes around their necks and needed reminding that these volunteers were indeed all healthy. If you apply the lessons learned from this experience to a nursing-home environment, you can easily see how minor discomforts take on overwhelming stressful proportions while helplessness and resignation set in.

The active old, on the other hand, resist the temptation to give in to such habits. What you see in them is the result of a lifetime of building up good habits of effective stress management. They do not dwell on problems. They have a positive, forward-looking attitude with plenty of social and intellectual stimulation and a good sense of humor that stops stress in its tracks. They follow a life of routine and structure. This helps them sleep well at night. Up and about during the day, they really have never stopped working, even though it may not be the job they did for most of their lives, and they may not be paid for it. Their reward is that they enjoy every single minute of living. Their biggest asset – they do not think about their age.

Asked how old I am I have to think back at the year I was born and calculate from there. A lesson in stress management comes from the study of centenarians by Thomas Perls, Director of the New England Centenarian Study at Beth Israel Deaconess medical center in Boston. He defines the "oldest old as being over 95. " In their nineties they were essentially problem-free. As nonagenarians, many were employed, were sexually active and enjoyed the outdoors and the arts." "Problem-free" is what we all aspire to and what you have to look forward to.

People over 80 to 85, having survived or escaped most diseases, are often healthier and more active than many who are younger. The number of Americans aged 100 or more has doubled since 1980, and four out of five of them are women. There are at present around 72,000 centenarians across the United States, and the projection forecasts that by 2050 there will be around 1 million. In France, in 2010 there were, 7,662 centenarians, compared with 200 in 1953. How will they deal with stress?

I think of those over 80 as falling into two general groups — those who are active participants in society and those who are not. The active old may be 80, 90,100 or more but do not look, behave or show physical changes that have been associated with their chronological age. They usually are physically active and have probably been so all their lives. Above all, they have developed excellent stress- coping skills.

What to Do About It

- Be physically active
- Practice good coping skills
- Participate actively in your community
- Have good health , eat well sleep well
- Do not generate or quickly dismiss your own stress.
- Maintain your general health habits.

Whatever you do, maintain a sense of humor. See and share the funny side of the situation. Lighten things up. Open the window, play some music, laugh, sing, cry and stress will be relieved.

Sacrifice is not a useful outcome for anyone.

REFLECTIONS

- Do you look to the future and how to best manage what's coming, even turning it into a positive.   Y/N
- Rate each of these sources of stress in your life (where 1 is 'low stress' and 5 is 'high stress'):
  Money ( ) Health ( ) Family ( ) Work/life conflicts ( ) Retirement ( ) Care Giving ( ) Loss/Grieving ( ) Sex ( ) Moving house ( ) Change in job ( ) Lost your job ( ) Loss of Mobility/Independence ( ) Other
  _____

- Do you need to put more effort into your relationships with friends and relatives.   Y/N
- Could you sit less and be more active throughout the day.   Y/N
- What are a few things you could do starting today to improve the quality of your sleep. _____
  _____

- List the aspects of your life to which you now intend to give more attention: _____
  _____

FOUR | How Stress-Fit Are You

J ust as you try to keep yourself *physically-fit* by being active, by exercising, think of keeping yourself *stress-fit* by adopting good stress-management habits.

Yet there are no '*stress-fitness gyms©*'. There are no '*Stress-Watchers*'© groups, like Weight-Watchers for group support. Where do you begin? How can you assess where you stand in your stress skills? What works for you? Which new skills will help you live a better life? Should you shed some and adopt others?

Mindful stress-reduction centers provide effective training to deal with stress. This book's *Tool-kit* gives you many options. Yet stress-fitness is more than that.

As we get older we are supposed to grow wiser. In your 20s you believe you know it all. As you get older you are more likely to listen to others. Your first 50 years have conditioned you physically, emotionally and financially for the balance of your life. You have acquired a load of habits, good and bad, and expectations. You have the ability to change – to adapt your expectations of what might happen.

Whether you are 20, 30 or 50 years old, life has presented you with unique challenges that are quite different at each stage. First it might be getting an education, looking for a job, tackling your education debts, keeping your lust manageable. Then in your 30s, a partner, family, perhaps children, balancing work and family, child care, acquiring a home and moving up in your job. By 50 years you may be an empty-nester, balancing work and care-giving of an older parent, reassessing where you are and what you expect out of the rest of your life. At each stage you have faced and handled stress with varying degrees of success. Either way, you have developed a Data Base, 50 years of experience. How did you cope? What has your relationship to stress been? Did you cope effectively or can you learn a thing or two. You cannot change everything all at once.

Stress affects people in so many different ways because *we* are all different. Our basic state of health changes with age as do our attitudes. The history of our coping habits, the way we dealt with each stress encounter, stored in our Data Base is recalled with each new event. As a result our stress threshold may be high or low. This all comes to bear in defining our stress-fitness. Each one of us has along the way learned different ways of reacting. Some of us bite our nails, show nervous twitches or laugh nervously. Others are cool and relaxed and may even see the funny side of a situation. We are all different. Each one of us reacts differently to stress, even members of the same family.

Our first 50 years of experience, every stress encounter, gave us skills, taught us habits. We can at any time do better on our health habits and physical fitness. We can also use help in our relationship with stress. If you do not learn to manage stress, it can be a silent killer. Even if it does not kill, it can cause heart attacks, stroke, Type II diabetes, obesity, cancer, depression, dementia, and bring on signs of aging earlier. For evidence, compare before and after photographs of US Presidents of the past 50 years.

WHAT IS STRESS FITNESS?

We know about exercise fitness – basic muscle tone is essential to your ability to react to a physical demand. Just as there are many ways of being physically fit with stronger muscles, flexibility, balance and endurance, so there are many aspects to being stress-fit.

As with exercise, you need frequent, low level stress to maintain responsiveness to a sudden stress challenge – to manage stress. In this way you avoid reaching destructive consequences of oxidative stress and outpouring of damaging hormones. By appreciating where you are on this scale and your stress threshold at any one time, you are better able to manage stress, to draw on your best state of health and experience to respond – your stress-fitness.

ADAPTATION

Stress-Fitness is not so much about the stresses we face but the process we use to manage them. We call it coping. The key to managing stress is the ability to adapt, to retain what is good and dump what is not, to let go of guilt and grudges, sway with the punches, to be *responsive to change.* Our slate at 50 is not as clean as it was when we were born. Experiences of the first 50 years have etched programs in our brain and body that we need to assess, retain, reinforce or erase if need be. On being faced with a stressful experience, how do we confront it? Are we scared? Or is it just another thing to deal with? How long does it take us to get over it or do we have trouble shedding it?

On the other hand with age also comes a sense of freedom. You may say "No" as often as it suits you. You may sleep any time at all or dance all night even if alone in your living room. How we respond to stress from this day forward depends on us rather than the event. And that means being aware of where we are at this point in time both physically and emotionally. Are we at peace with who we are and how we feel? If not, we can change things.

MANAGE IT

There are four basic ways of managing stress:

1. COPE EFFECTIVELY. You analyze and control how you respond to keep the stress response within manageable limits — within the normal range and duration. *Stop the stress* in its tracks if you have generated it, solve the problem, prepare for a successful speech or event, plan ahead for retirement, board up your home before a hurricane, make and keep friends to have them when you need them, talk to your family, save even during retirement, or resolve a difficult dilemma in a personal relationship. These are all examples of effective coping.

What to Do About It

- Stop, count to 10, breathe deeply and slowly, calm down. Analyze and process what is happening.
- Catch yourself whenever negative thoughts creep in and stop them.
- Delete *What if* stress that is beyond your immediate control.
- *Be prepared* if you possibly can by anticipating what you might need when you have to take action. Do your homework before a presentation or stock up on essentials before a power failure.
- *Do not allow your stress to build up.* Do everything in your power to avoid or reduce the excessive outpouring of hormones that can cause damage. Relax. Take frequent time-outs.
- *Allow yourself quiet time to pause and recover*
- *Learn stress- relieving skills from your Tool-Kit*

2. PARTIALLY EFFECTIVE COPING. You do something that defuses the stress response though the action is not directly related to the stress. Examples are various forms of exercise especially ones that dispel frustration, such as burning pent-up energy from anxiety by hitting a golf or tennis ball. Or they can be any form of exercise that distracts you or requires your total attention such as surfing, skiing, cycling, sailing. It could also be one that makes you feel good about yourself — a walk, a swim, going to the gym, a yoga class, or just the fact you did something. It can even be something that leaves you with a sense of accomplishment like digging up that root in your garden, mowing the lawn, gardening, even house-cleaning, or maybe calling someone you have neglected.

Partially effective coping is a useful tool when we want to pause and regroup before tackling something bigger. It can dispel anger.

What to Do About It

- Do something physical to expend energy in a satisfying way unrelated to the stress like going for a swim or taking a warm bath or massage.
- Breathe deeply and exhale slowly to slow down your heart rate and calm you.
- Close your left nostril with your thumb, inhale deeply through the right nostril, then close your right nostril and exhale through the left.

3. DEFERRED COPING You put off the response to the stress temporarily by some diverting action. It could include a physical reaction as simple as taking some deep breaths, lowering your shoulders, stretching or saying to yourself "I shall deal with it in 15 minutes" by which time the threat may have moved on. Or you realized that it was one of those self-generated stresses, a 'What if' worry that was not real at all or that you could do nothing about right away. Like partially effective coping it gives you a chance to pause and collect your thoughts.

4. INEFFECTUAL COPING is also unrelated to the stress. It is the worst and most common way of confronting a stress yet it includes reactions that many of us indulge in like anger. It

may reduce the stress response but has a downside that may be worse than the stress itself. We may do something socially unacceptable, harmful to ourselves or someone else. They often include aggression.

We each develop favorite ineffectual coping behaviors that are the opposite of being Stress-Fit. They do not work in managing the stress because they are not aimed at the cause of the stress itself. These behaviors fall into two broad categories, aggression and pleasure-seeking.

Aggression/Anger

Domestic violence, insult, road rage, shouting, breaking things, spanking a crying child, stepping on the pedal or walking out on family. It is most often harmful to oneself, drinking, pill or social drug-taking, smoking or overeating to dull the stress; some call it 'numbing the pain' though there may be no physical pain involved or suicide. Compulsive behaviors like picking at hair or skin, nail-biting, indiscriminate shopping especially of things you do not need, gambling, computer games, excessive talking on the telephone when it does not seem warranted. These all exemplify ineffectual coping.

Withdrawing to bed, avoiding social contact or not answering the phone are all behaviors used to escape, or avoid facing up to the problem that caused the stress in the first place.

In the late 1960s, I was studying how the brain and the pituitary-adrenal system respond to various types of chronic and acute stress. At the same time, my colleagues at Stanford University, in California, Bob Conner and Seymour Levine, were doing research into aggressive behavior.

In our research, a rat receiving a mild electric shock to its feet would jump and lick its paws. A pair of rats receiving the same shock resorted to attacking each other, presumably thinking the other guy did it! The number of attacks was used to measure aggression. I measured the stress responses in these animals, fully expecting that fighting would add further stress to that of the electric shock. Yet when the animals had another rat to attack, they showed much lower stress hormone responses than when they got shocked alone. After doing everything we could to exclude other interpretations, we concluded that fighting represented a way of *coping*. It was ineffectual, though, since fighting did nothing to change the duration of the shock or relieve its intensity. It may however have reduced the pain.

We humans indulge in many aggressive coping behaviors, thinking it will help to "let it out": bursting out in anger, smashing dishes, physically or verbally abusing a spouse, punching someone who annoys us, daubing a wall with graffiti, damaging public property. Benefit from these behaviors is doubtful; the harm can be huge. Addictive behaviors such as gambling or compulsive shopping on e-Bay may seem innocent but have far-reaching financial debt potential that easy access to credit cards and the internet provide. Such behaviors can place an intolerable strain on family relationships and put at risk one's job and financial independence.

It can also be damaging to health. Anger and hostility are documented killers, increasing the risk of heart disease. Research has shown that angry people have an increased output of stress hormones, causing higher blood pressure and increased heart rate. A study of young lawyers carried out in their late fifties was followed up 25 years later. Those who had high hostility were four to five times more likely to develop coronary heart disease later in life. Of those who at the age of 24 had been assessed as being angry, 20% had died by the age of 50.

Pleasure Seeking

Ineffectual coping habits include pleasure-seeking – what is wrong with that, you may ask? Psychologists studying happiness have observed a marked difference between pleasure and happiness. Pleasure is temporary and its effects wear off. While we may feel great upon arriving at a luxury hotel for a few days' vacation, by the third day we have habituated to our new environment and start to feel bored, find fault with the hotel or worry that we are spending too much money.

During my undergraduate years I played on the doubles table-tennis team. My partner was an excellent player and a lot of fun as long as he had had his dose of hashish. However, he was abominably quarrelsome of he missed his dose as he did sometimes when running late. When we indulge in pleasure-seeking activities such as eating, gambling, drinking, use of recreational drugs such as cocaine, a variety of narcotics and/ or stimulants, we may feel better temporarily, but we have not solved any problems. In fact we have often made them worse.

Such solutions to stress can harm both the individual and those around them. Coffee, alcohol and smoking are frequently used to boost confidence. Prescription drugs such as sleeping or pain pills, anxiety medications, even anesthetics as in the famous Michael Jackson case, round off the list. The ultimate example of self-damaging behavior is suicide – the inability to cope with stress.

TO BE STRESS-FIT USE YOUR BRAIN

Your brain is your computer. The entire process of evaluating an event and dismissing it or responding to it as a stressful threat happens in a split second. Your brain receives information that something has changed in the surrounding world or the brain itself generates a worrying thought. The hypothalamus then scans the Data Base in the hippocampus. How the hypothalamus responds depends on whether the situation was expected, predictable and controllable, the degree to which the person believes he or she is in control.

The process of analyzing an incoming stress is represented in Table 2. Using this Table you can work out, for example, on the first line, that if you are expecting an event, such as moving to a new house, if this is not your first move, with a good previous experience when you coped well, you are more likely to handle this new move effectively. But if, as on the second line, this is your first move, you have never moved before or you are giving up a home you love so much, you may focus on the loss of the house and you may not feel able to cope. Your brain will register this reaction in your Data Base as an unpleasant, negative, stressful experience. It is up to you to find the positives in any situation and focus on them. You may use this Table to determine how well you might cope in different circumstances or turn negatives into positives.

Table 2: How Severe Will the Stress Be?

Expect Event?	Experienced Before?	How Coped?	Feel Able to Cope?	Stress Response	Feedback to Data Base
Yes	Yes	Well	Yes	0 — low	Positive
Yes	Yes	Well	not now	high	Negative
Yes	No	no data	Yes	medium	Positive
Yes	No	no data	No	high	Negative
No	Yes	Well	Yes	0 — low	Positive
No	Yes	Well	not now	high	Negative
No	No	no data	Yes	Medium	Positive
No	No	no data	No	very high	Negative

Turn every stress into a positive experience.

If you have fair warning such as an act of nature, at least make sure you do everything to prepare for it. If you are stressed and irritated by the long security lines at airports, make sure you remind yourself that they are for your protection. If your bridge partner is not concentrating perhaps she is going through a rough patch, so think how you may help or how lucky you are to be playing bridge at all instead of sitting alone at home and how fortunate it is to be able to exercise your brain or, through bridge, have a circle of friends.

Build up your Data Base.

Failures and successes are fed back into the Data Base. A stress that was previously handled well may become more stressful if conditions have changed — if, for example, a person feels incapacitated by age, illness, sleep deprivation, or feelings of helplessness. Every major failure to cope with stress is fed back into the database, and as a result future responses to a stressful event can produce excessive responses within the system — the sign of an inability to cope. The reverse is true. Every successful coping with a perceived stress reinforces with positive feedback the database so that future responses are attenuated. The solution is to replace the failures in the data base with successes. You can do this by learning effective coping skills. This is the way you program your brain to cope with stress instead of letting it be programmed haphazardly by what someone else says or even by what your own imagination or dreams slip into it.

Well-managed, stress is beneficial.

Stress has come to have negative connotations, but it is crucial for survival. Without it, the body would not be able to maintain homeostasis — the state of chemical equilibrium reached within the body. You need small, frequent, manageable stimuli that provoke the stress response in order to keep your body tuned and in balance. Stress management does not mean abolishing all stress from our lives; it means finding ways to cope with stress levels that are not out of limits and would otherwise harm you.

YOU CAN DO IT

Believing you can control a situation is the first step towards actually doing so. This is as true for animals as it is for people.

Mice given an electric shock develop ulcers. But if they learn that pushing a lever can terminate the shock, their ulcers go away. They continue to get fewer ulcers even if the lever is completely disconnected from the shock device and the shocks still come through despite their efforts. The opposite happens, too. Guinea pigs placed in a box in which histamine is sprayed get an asthma attack. They then continue having asthma attacks every time they are in the box, even when no histamine is present. Do you recognize yourself shying away from situations that are no longer real?

Talk, Touch and Socialize

The power of the psychological element is frequently ignored in clinical trials. For more than twenty years it had been generally agreed that lying continuously in bed is stressful, since more of the stress hormone cortisol was found in the urine of the volunteers. But our research provided new clues into ways of reducing this stress — and a fascinating slant on the differences between the sexes. In 1982, we did our first head-down bed-rest study using women volunteers. To my surprise, I found that after a rise on the first day, due to being in a new and unusual environment, their cortisol levels showed no further increase, and even went into a slight decline. This was not true for men where it stayed high throughout.

When we selected volunteers to take part in our studies, we always gave them a detailed briefing about exactly what would happen. This was taped, and we did not deviate in practice from what we told them. On the morning we briefed our first women volunteers, I distinctly remember the hubbub of voices in the conference room. Sixty women, from all walks of life and who had never set eyes on one another, were socializing and chatting up a storm. With men, we had invariably met a quiet and muted audience.

The eight women finally selected were mostly professionals — an attorney, a nurse, a radiation technician, and a travel agent among them. They came in with definite plans about how they would spend their time and what goals they expected to accomplish. They also talked a lot about various aspects of the study. This was distinctly different from the behavior of our male volunteers, who did not talk about their feelings unless asked to, and even then very reluctantly. Mostly, men tended to talk about sports and money.

With the next study, I tried a little psychological experiment. The few men who had taken part in previous studies were asked to act as unofficial mentors to first-timers. Then we paired them up in rooms with the rookies we had selected. No increase in cortisol excretion was seen in any men this time nor in any later studies using this approach. They had reduced their stress levels simply by venting their concerns — just as the women had done.

There is more to the social element than friendship and communication at which women in general excel. Studies have now shown that married men live longer than single ones while that does not apply to single women. Whereas the best thing a man can do for his health is being married to a woman, the best thing a woman can do for her health is nurture her relationships with her girl-friends. Physically, 'girl-time' results in more serotonin being secreted, the neurotransmitter that helps combat depression, as well as oxytocin the nurturing hormone. Women share feelings and do more touching, kissing and hugging as they relate to other women. Unsuccessful marriages inevitably are those that are deprived of touching, not necessarily sex. Societies that are more touchy-feely, such as Mediterranean cultures, tend to live longer, healthier lives.

Face Up to Age

The stresses we face typically change with age. The ability to keep some sense of personal control is eroded by other peoples' attitudes, as well as by physical slowing down. Something as minor as the need for reading glasses can become a major blow to one's sense of independence. It can affect one's ability to drive, for one thing. My solution was having my lenses replaced with cataract surgery. Even more serious are the three most likely events that come with getting older — retirement, loss of a significant other, and relocation.

Relocation, to an assisted living facility in particular, is with few exceptions a one-way street. Residents in nursing homes often have very high cortisol levels, similar to those found in patients suffering from depression. Acquiring coping skills and learning how to perceive that they have greater control of their lives reduces their cortisol levels to normal and improves their general well-being.

Another successful approach to developing coping skills that you can try yourself was developed by Florence Clark at the University of Southern California. Although she calls it "occupational therapy for independent older adults," it is essentially comprised of coping skills that are tailored to the individual. She studied 361 persons over the age of sixty for several months. One example was "an eighty-year-old woman who was depressed and spent most of her days in bed or watching television. She rarely ventured out of her building because she was unfamiliar with public transportation and was afraid of falling when taking that first big step to climb aboard a bus."

The therapist identified the problem as the size of the step. She provided a step to practice on that was of similar height to that from the street onto the bus. She also helped the subject with her first trips out on the bus and then directed her to try it on her own. The woman reported later that she felt healthier and regained her sense of independence. Other persons of the same age in the study who were given equal time and attention for social activities, such as games, movies, or craft projects, showed no improvement.

Freedom

In contrast to disadvantages, I found a tremendous sense of freedom when I first crossed that 50 line. You may take up a new sport, wear a bright color, be venturesome. You have attained recognition and can now enjoy it. You feel free to say 'No' to an unreasonable request in a way you did not earlier in your career. Frankly, you care less about what others think of you and more about how you feel about yourself. The sense of freedom comes from not feeling you have to try harder to impress others but mostly to be yourself, express yourself, enjoy what you do and how well you do it. Add that to your Data Base!

Avoid It

Avoiding a problem rather than addressing it — otherwise known as procrastination — is a common example of a non-coping behavior. If you put off going to the ophthalmologist or the dentist because you are worried about what the visit may reveal, all you are doing is adding to your stress by conjuring up problems that may be far worse than the facts warrant.

During the 2010 Census, many seniors put off filling out their forms, worrying that the information might be misused. An annual avoidance ritual has grown up around the requirement to file income tax returns — as evidenced by the rush to the post office at the last possible moment.

In its most serious forms, avoidance can result in *freezing,* the loss of the ability either to fight or to flee. Sufferers from this extreme form of procrastination will stay in bed or sleep all day, escaping to a fantasy-land staring at the TV or a computer for hours without really watching.

Addiction

Research into the relationship between addictions – drugs, sleeping pills, sugar, alcohol, tobacco, gambling, compulsive shopping, even work – and the stress response is opening up huge possibilities for understanding both processes and finding new ways of treating them. Underlying both is the basic need to numb the putative pain on the way to feeling good.

An important issue in drug dependency is craving, an intense desire to re-experience the effects of the drug. People who have stopped taking drugs, alcohol or smoking always find that the craving continues long after the habit is discontinued.

Research shows that the craving is closely related to the release of the body's own opiate endorphins, or painkillers. The drug Naltrexone, which counteracts the effects of opiates such as morphine or heroin, was surprisingly found to decrease the craving for cocaine and alcohol as well. Exactly how this works is not yet clear, but this treatment provides a new way to help prevent 'cured' addicts from relapsing. On the other hand, stress or the release of the hormone CRH in the hypothalamus, which initiates the stress response, can restore craving. CRH, which also raises anxiety, is increased in the brain of addicts who are attempting to break free from their habit.

Addiction has many forms. It can involve drugs, nicotine, alcohol, overeating, anorexia, bulimia (overeating followed by vomiting) and even compulsive behaviors such as nail-biting, incessant hand-washing, compulsive neatness, or excessive exercising. Any activity that is done obsessively, gambling, playing the stock market, shopping for things we do not want or need, spending hours at a time watching videos or web surfing — falls into the category of ineffective coping solutions. The electronic devices that have flooded the market, social websites and other forms of communication have in fact reduced social interaction. As with other addictions, these behaviors produce physical withdrawal symptoms when stopped, and often the stoppage is soon followed by a relapse. For example, excessive eaters who diet feel deprived. Just like drug addicts they know how easy it is to relapse.

Equally, although exercise is good for you and is needed at all ages, obsessive exercising is an addiction and can be damaging. It is a case of excessive stress with damaging oxidative consequences. It is not unlike overusing gravity such as the hyper-gravity that would be experienced by spinning very rapidly on a centrifuge or pulling high G on an aircraft or driving a fast car. Male rats living at 2 G have smaller testes and lower levels of the sex hormone testosterone.

Male marathon runners show a reduced production of testosterone and women marathoners often stop menstruating. If they discontinue exercising for any reason, they go through withdrawal symptoms, feeling sluggish, unwell, and depressed. It has been suggested that this may be due to the craving for the pleasurable high from the stress hormones and endorphins, the natural morphine-like substances released by daily exercise. Risk-taking and thrill-seeking taken to excess may become obsessive or addictive.

The sense of security from staying in familiar places reduces uncertainty. When visiting us in London from Athens, my uncle and aunt Calypso always stayed at the same hotel, in the same room, year in year out. Her first job was to clean the insides of every cupboard and drawer and to clean them again before she left. The hotel staff loved them because in addition to doing their work for them, they left a good tip. Throughout her life, her biggest delight was to be given a box of something to clean or the silver to polish.

Addictions have downsides, even in something apparently good or innocuous like exercise or housecleaning when taken to excess.

Share It

Your appraisal of a situation may bring on an emotional response ranging from excitement and happiness to fear, guilt, or anxiety. This will influence the choice of coping strategy you adopt. If you want to lighten the burden, share it.

Moving house may raise physical concerns of packing, financial worries, and the emotional turmoil of going through and disposing of mementos. All told, the task is daunting and stressful. Do not expect to do it all at the same time and by yourself. Separate each aspect of the move. Organize what needs to be done before you even start and allow plenty of time to accomplish each task. Seek help or advice even if you do not follow it. Others may have creative ideas. Throw a pot-luck party where friends come to do specific tasks around the house. Allow yourself a break to relax or take a walk.

Speaking to a group of nurse caregivers and their boss who was seeking ways to motivate them, I asked what they would appreciate most as recognition. "Half a day off!" was the unanimous reply to the surprise of their boss who was big on handing out certificates of recognition.

Taking a break to recover is an important practice to adopt. Sacrifice is not a useful outcome for anyone.

REFLECTIONS

- Do you accept new challenges but are okay saying no to more than you can handle?   Y/N
- Do you tend to address the stresses in your life before letting them build up?   Y/N
- When feeling stressed and run down do you make an effort to get extra sleep?   Y/N

- Are you quickly able to notice when you become hooked by a negative emotion?   Y/N
- Do you use your breath to help you calm down?   Y/N
- Do you find it difficult asking others for help?   Y/N
- Do you tend to dwell on what tomorrow may bring?
                                                                                        Y/N
- Do you find it hard to develop a new habit?   Y/N
- Do you catch yourself saying "I'm too old to _____," then step back to consider why you are thinking that?
                                                                                        Y/N
- Are you excited to learn new things and face new challenges?   Y/N
- List the most valuable skills and/or habits you have developed in your life to this point that help you deal with stressful situations and people? _____
  _____
  _____

- List any ways you regularly cope with stress in an ineffectual way: _____
  _____

- On a scale of 1 – 10 (where 10 is best) how would you rate your stress fitness? _____

FIVE | **Your Stress Tool-Kit**

Your Tool-Kit gives you a wealth of options to turn to when you feel stressed. Having a hard time managing everyday stress? Looking for a little more inner peace? No matter what's causing you stress in your life, finding strategies to relax during busy or difficult times can give your body and mind a chance to calm down and recuperate.

There are things you can do right away to get instant relief. Calm down. Focus on the present. Then, there is the slower process changing your mind-set. The latter entails processing information, decision-making, response and feeding your data base with positive experiences; in other words what you perceive as a stress and how you respond to it.

Turn stress into a joyful event – play, smile, laugh.

Most bathrooms have a First-Aid Kit. How about a Stress Emergency Kit? What if we lose our wallet with all our credit cards? Do we have all the phone numbers on hand to call? Do we save money for that rainy day? Do we keep candles and matches handy or batteries for your flashlight in case of a power failure? Do we have a small reserve fridge for use before an important dinner party or during the long Christmas holiday? How do we respond to unwanted telephone solicitation calls trying to make us feel guilty? The list is endless and we can reduce self-imposed stress by careful planning. Walk things through with worst case scenarios. Quietly, you can assess if you 'want to go there.'

You can use the instant relief techniques to relax immediately giving you enough time to pause and reassess the situation. Reprogramming takes longer; it is the long-term solution that you want to aim for.

INSTANT RELIEF

There are certain physical ways that can help give you in-stant relief when you feel overwhelmed with stress. Even when you are about to enter a situation that you anticipate will be stressful you can prepare yourself with these simple maneuvers.

It is easier to recognize tell-tale stress signs in others than in ourselves. Look around you and you will know what I mean. When the Sunday sermon was boring I used to do my field-testing by watching out for signs in the congregation. How many men had tensed up necks and shoulders? Were they restlessly playing with their ring till it was time for that cigarette? Frowning, yawning, fidgeting, red face, scrunched-up shoulders, tight jaw, hyperventilating, twitching, finger-tapping, restless leg syndrome sometimes known as St.Vitus dance are some of many signs of brewing stress. Picking up stress signs in others will help you become more aware when you experience stress yourself. What do *you* do in these situations? Take steps and check its progress.

Got a minute? Here are some techniques for instant stress-relief:

Deep Belly Breathing

Your body has its own-stress relieving mechanism – breathing. Sit or stand up straight, shoulders down, with your hands on your tummy, chest pushed upward. Most exercises tell you to tightly suck in your belly muscles. Here you do the opposite — let your belly muscles out. Inhale deeply without raising your shoulders; it is not easy to do with shoulders raised. Feel the air all the way down into your belly. We normally breathe with shallow breaths into our upper chest and increase adrenaline and anxiety. Here it is the opposite: deep belly breathing and slow inhalation force relaxation. Form an "O" with your mouth and exhale while sighing loudly. Imagine all those worries drifting out of your body along with the sound. This is when you should contract those belly muscles tightly to get all that air out. You have surely heard tennis stars like Maria Sharapova shriek and groan while serving. This noisy exhalation affords split second relaxation to fuel all her strokes. Stress won't stand a chance against the relaxing power of deep, cleansing breaths. Now go ahead…and just breathe.

The Jaw Trick

It may look foolish, but there is no way you can avoid being relaxed with your jaw open. You cannot even frown with your jaw open. Try it! Then ask yourself, "Could things be worse?" They always can.

I taught the jaw trick to my NASA colleague Bob Rhome. Sitting across the table at directors' meetings, I would "watch" his blood pressure rise. After catching his eye, I would drop my jaw as daintily as I could. He would promptly reciprocate, trying to hold back a smile. The stress was defused.

To get maximal benefit of this jaw release, place the palms of your hands on your cheeks with thumbs behind your ear lobes. Hold for a few minutes. Now relax your jaw looking straight ahead. Relax your eyes, eyebrows, cheeks and jaw. Doing this, forces you to relax the rest of your body. Tightening your jaw and clenching the teeth makes the rest of your body seize up as well. If you watch runners race, you can tell if they are seizing up because instead of leaning forward as they do when they are relaxed, they start leaning back.

People who clench fists and grind their teeth while asleep get relief by wearing a gum-shield. A practical example of the stress relief a gum-shield can provide was the recent case of 34-year-old Italian golfer Edoardo Molinari, who had to suspend playing because of excruciating pain in his left wrist from tendonitis. Neither massage, laser treatment nor plain rest brought relief. Finally, a chiropractor suggested he wear a gum-shield while playing and when exercising in the gym with miraculous success. The gum-shield helps him close his mouth properly and prevents the tightening of the muscles in the left upper side of his body. Chewing gum can give similar relief.

Neck and Shoulder Release

Invariably, tight neck muscles and scrunched-up shoulders are a sure sign of accumulated stress. Massage and relaxation do help but here is a simple technique I found useful especially when sitting in front of the computer begins to take its toll. Squeeze tightly your shoulders up to your ears, hold for a count of 10 while breathing normally and drop them. Bend your arms at the elbows and grasp them behind your back pulling them down ward. Make sure you head does not lean forward and your chest is turned upward. Your shoulders will be pulled down automatically and you will feel some tenderness in your back muscles. Hold as long as you can and release.

If you are at your computer make sure you are sitting upright. With your arms at right angle, slide your elbows back as far as you can. Continue breathing normally and hold this to a slow count of 12 while feeling your shoulder blades squeezed together. Release.

Stand Up and Stretch

Stretching is a very important component of relaxing, especially as we age and tend to become stiffer. Stand Up as often as you can and stretch your arms up to the sky. Stretching a tight muscle releases the tension. The simple act of getting up from your bed in the morning or from a chair has been shown to increase brain blood flow. If it did not you would faint and lose consciousness.

It is a good habit to stretch whenever you can; first thing in the morning and all day long. Try some gentle stretching every day. Swimming, too, is an excellent way to relax joints and wash away muscle tension. So is taking a warm bath. Make a ritual of it. Use sweet-smelling bath salts or relaxing magnesium salts if you desire or sniff a drop of your favorite aromatic oil.

Touch Someone

Touching someone with the palm of your hand is a calming, reassuring gesture. The palm of your hand rather than your fingertips has calming sensors.

For many cultures touching, patting someone on the knee or back are quite friendly and normal, as is walking arm in arm in public. Other cultures consider touching inappropriate so be aware before you do it. This has been particularly true since sexual harassment has made touching illegal.

Hug

There is nothing quite as calming and comforting as a warm, sincere hug at a time of loss or to dispel stress. Just as you can judge a person's personality from their handshake, you can measure a person's sincerity from the way they hug. Are you dating someone? You can tell a lot about them by the way they hug or even if they hug.

Pause

Any relaxation technique gives you a time-out from whatever stress you are facing. The basic relaxation technique is to set aside a few minutes of quiet time. Sit down without slouching, but in a comfortable, relaxed position, hands resting on your thighs. Breathe in deeply through the nose to the count of four, and then exhale slowly through the mouth until you feel that you have emptied your lungs. Repeat this three to four times. Close your eyes, let the muscles go limp (as well as the jaw), and relax your whole body.

Visualize yourself resting in a calm, favorite place. Allow yourself to fully experience all sights and sounds of that blissful haven for a few minutes. When you are ready, take a deep breath, open your eyes, and think of yourself as refreshed and energized. Stretch gently.

Cry

Have you noticed how wonderfully calm you feel after a really good cry. It's Nature's stress release.

Crying comes more easily to some people than others. That is a blessing. We usually associate crying with sadness. We cry about the loss of someone including your pet. We do not cry about losing our keys or glasses.

Grief has more to do with what the loss does to us than the departed. How dare they leave us? However old we are our feelings are hurt when we are left alone or perhaps orphaned even after 50. Crying even at the loss of someone else in a good movie is very therapeutic.

Crying and laughing are healthy ways of relieving stress and helping you address decisions. The tears you shed because you are sad release chemicals that your body is trying to get rid of. Think of it as taking out the trash so that your body will feel better. Don't keep that trash around. Cry if you need to.

Laugh

Do not forget to laugh. It's the great healer. You do not stop laughing just because you are older. Lee Berk at Loma Linda University, in California, showed that *happy, silly* laughter, in contrast to *pretend* laughter, reduces stress-hormone levels and boosts the immune system. Best-selling author Norman Cousins brought attention to the health benefits of laughter in his book *The Anatomy of an Illness*, published in 1991. Bedridden and weak, suffering with ankylosing spondylitis, a degenerative connective-tissue disease, he discovered he could only sleep after watching Candid Camera and Marx Brothers films. He also noticed he was in less pain. He had been given a one-in-five-hundred chance of recovery, but somehow he eventually did recover, and he attributed it to the healing effects of laughter.

The idea was explored in a five-year study at UCLA entitles "Rx Laughter" in which researchers evaluated the impact of laughter in both healthy and very sick children. Much like Cousins, they were using vintage comedy of Chaplin, Abbott and Costello, W. C. Fields, Buster Keaton, and the Marx Brothers, which is completely fresh to these kids.

Bill Marx, son of Harpo Marx, says of the project: "When you have a sense of humor, you automatically have an option on your view of life." Ronald J. Fields, grandson of W. C. Fields, comments: "Humor is nothing but extreme positive thinking." Psychologist Margery Silver, who collaborated with Tom Perls on The New England Centenarian study, observed that centenarians often have a great sense of humor, finding it in ordinary things. She says they found that "laughter is like internal jogging."

Music is Therapy

As long as it is the right kind, music is a great stress soother. Studies have found that tunes, dating from when the individual was a young person, are the best, particularly in those with senility or dementia. The beat should be close to a person's normal heart rate and preferably something the person usually enjoys. But fast, loud music can be stressful.

Singing appears to be particularly beneficial to health. In the 1960s, a popular TV show was "Sing Along with Mitch." It featured band leader Mitch Miller and a "follow the bouncing ball" set of lyrics on the screen. Viewers who sang along at home may not have realized that in addition to having fun they were reducing stress and improving their health. John Sparks, former vice president at the American Symphony Orchestra League, points to an increasing number of studies in persons 55 and over that revealed significant benefits of singing to health.

Using surveys and questionnaires, one study in England noted that 79% of participants felt less stressed, while another at the University of California, Irvine found choristers had intensely improved immune responses both before and after singing. Many community and church choirs are open to all who wish to join. If you don't want to commit to regular rehearsals, just invite some friends over for a sing-along to your favorites!

Pray

We all pray at one time or another, whether we acknowledge it or not. When we say, "I wish the sun would come out" or

"I wish the pain would go away," that is prayer, because it is addressing a greater power in whose goodness and omnipotence we believe.

Prayer can be regarded as another form of meditation that calms, relaxes and relieves anxiety. Many people find comfort in prayer when facing distress, danger, or death. There are no atheists in foxholes or trenches.

Scientific research into the links between religious belief, health, and longevity has, however, been controversial. Individuals may draw strength, comfort, and a sense of security from faith in a greater power without being regular churchgoers. However, congregations of all faiths are an invaluable source of support and community, especially to those who live alone.

Play

Play, feeling good and happiness seem to go hand in hand. Play gets you out of the rut of worrying, feeling down or sorry for yourself. Too old to play? Not at all. Look up septuagenarian Stephen Jepson who has made it his life's purpose to encourage everyone at any age to continue playing. His latest achievement is teaching himself how to juggle!

Worrying about looking foolish to others? Who cares? Go to the playground and swing on a swing. Turn up the music and dance on your own or join a group. In the small town of Chati in France, the local nursing home partnered with Nintendo to set up play stations. "We were looking for physical activities that could be done by people with limited mobility" said social director, Aurelie Retif. Wheelchair-bound residents shake and point the remote at skittles in the virtual-world bowling alley.

Learning how to use the controls provides an obvious sense of achievement, mental stimulation and coordination. Sharing fun with friends relieves stress and the company is an added bonus. Play has also been shown to increase empathy among persons with pain whereas stress reduces empathy (Martin LJ et al. 2015). Ever noticed when a stranger calls up for a contribution? When you are stressed-out you are less likely to feel generous? On the other hand if you have the chance to play with them, to meet them face to face, your generosity and empathy increases.

Take a walk

Make a habit of taking a walk once-a-day outside. A walk in the woods rejuvenates the mind and improves the ability to pay attention and focus. But even going around the block briskly with a bounce in your step, clears your mind and gives you a chance to take a break from whatever you were doing. No need for company. Look at whatever is around you; perhaps others are rushing by to get somewhere fast, looking frazzled and smile. Not you.

Exercise

Your mood influences how you feel and your perception of the seriousness of a stress. Increasing brain blood flow provides oxygen and nutrients to the brain. It affects mood and mental functions.

Aerobic exercise is a good example. It does not have to take a lot of time but it does need to be intense.

Equally your posture, how you sit or stand, can have a dramatic effect on how you feel. Dr Eric Peper at San Francisco State University asks his students to stand up 30 minutes into a class and wave their arms above their heads before sitting down again. He finds they experience great cognitive improvements and feel better. He also found that the way one sits can influence mood. Sitting up with good posture resulted in positive thoughts. Negative thoughts come with slouching.

LONG-TERM STRATEGIES

Be Prepared

There is much to learn from the intensive training astronauts undergo to prepare themselves for the numerous stressful circumstances they are likely to encounter.

They learn everything about their spacecraft: how it works, how it can malfunction, how to diagnose the fault and how to fix it, what constitutes an emergency, and where and when to seek help. They are physically very fit and, to escape a possible fire or a crash at landing, they practice dashing out of their spacecraft wearing their heavy space suits and running away for 100 yards as fast as they possibly can.

Russian cosmonauts go through training that is every bit as thorough. Its value was demonstrated on February 23, 1997, when technical problems beleaguered their Space Station *Mir*. The lithium perchlorate candles that provided life-giving oxygen were running low and one exploded. A dangerous fire filled the craft for several minutes with smoke. Despite choking smoke nobody panicked. The fire was put out and no one was seriously hurt. If you are ready to deal with a stressful situation, you are halfway to beating it. Being prepared can go a long way towards preventing anxiety.

ASTRONAUT WISDOM APPLIES ON EARTH

"In his book *An Astronaut's Guide to Life on Earth*, Chris Hadfield, former commander of the International Space Station (ISS), takes aim at the empty optimism of self-help books. Never mind thinking positive, he says — the real benefits come from preparing for the worst. This philosophy is common and necessary in space flight, and so, during 'contingency sims' simulations on the ground, NASA officials would throw a series of unexpected and unfortunate events at Hadfield and his fellow astronauts, to test their responses and to work out how they could be improved. Busy dealing with an already deadly technical threat to their lives in orbit, such as a medical emergency, the trainee spacemen and women would be told: oh, sorry, but now a fire has broken out. And by the way, you're leaking oxygen. Hadfield says he found it oddly comforting to be sitting around a table with friends and colleagues discussing, for example, how they would dispose of his corpse if he died in space."

On Earth, the same preparatory rules apply. However, Mother Nature is sometimes too great a force. My friends Jaye and Kathleen moved to a lovely home in balmy Florida only to find themselves in the path of hurricane Katrina followed by Wilma later on. In spite of boarding up the windows and taking shelter, there was nothing more they could do but wait it out and pray for minimal damage. This was not a stress they had brought on themselves. They had never experienced anything like it before. They did not know what to expect, how long it would last and what would be the aftermath. Dealing with the stress during the hurricane was one thing. Dealing afterwards with their own recovery as well as that of their property and their surroundings was quite another. The negative experience of helplessness against nature's force was bad enough. The stress was nerve-racking as weather forecasters described the path of the next hurricane and where it might land. Jaye says she knows why some people fall apart in those circumstances. Her advice, "you have to turn around and face it, and work very hard to overcome your stress even when feeling lousy." She adds, "it's all about feeling awful but dealing with it anyway."

Fear brought on by unfamiliar sounds during the night or some unknown person knocking at the door brings on a stress response. It is greater if you live alone. The feeling can be overcome or reduced if measures are taken to control the situation. Your peace of mind is less likely to be disturbed if you have a good security system, have access to a Call Button, a phone to call for help, and do not open the door to strangers.

By preparing carefully and being well informed, you can take the tension out of many situations. Knowing as much as you can about your subject and about your audience will reduce the stress of public speaking. Finding out about your potential employer before you go for a job interview, anticipating the questions you might be asked, preparing a well-laid-out résumé, and having hand-written material or well-organized visuals for a presentation will boost your confidence and reduce stress. In the same way, if you prepare for a visit with your doctor by organizing the questions that have been racing around your mind and making realistic observations of your symptoms, you are likely to experience the visit with much less stress as well as getting more out of it.

Fear of becoming incapacitated and needing care in your later years is a classic example of the need to prepare before being confronted with a snap decision made by others. You have made a will, haven't you? That's taking care of others when you no longer care. How about preparing for yourself?

Throughout life we need help from others but as we get older this need may increase. Make sure you communicate these needs and concerns early. Talk about them with your family or someone you can trust well before the time comes to make serious decisions about a change in your living conditions, from living by yourself to community or assisted living. This decision is hard to make for both of you. In discussing this issue, ask for more details of their concerns and expectations, how they assess your capabilities compared to how you do. Talking about it and the facts behind it will go a long way in reducing their stress as well as yours.

It might be really hard to ask for help, but it is very brave. Making such decisions is a bit like deciding to divorce. Divorce is a choice adults make for adult reasons and one of the most stressful things to deal with for everyone. It is hardest when the parties do not get along. Accept that some changes will happen. You may have to move or depend on a stranger to help you with your care. You'll get used to your new life sooner if you try to look at the positive aspects of it. Many problems may be part of the issue and you and others may have to change spending habits and expectations.

Talk to someone who has been through it. Recognize that each situation is different. Do the research yourself on the options so that you have the facts in any negotiations with your family and do not have to make a hasty decision. Making new friends can be scary but ultimately rewarding. There is always someone who can be your friend even in a care facility. Recruit a friend to be active with you. Ask them how they solved their disagreements. It is always useful to talk to someone. However, everyone makes mistakes in friendships. We say something we don't mean when we are tired or angry. Be willing to apologize. Practice being someone others want to be with.

Analyze

Be constantly on the alert when some stressful thought creeps into your brain and turns into fear, worry or anxiety. Get into the habit of questioning and analyzing any worrisome thought. Is it real? Take a quick time-out to analyze its real cause. Knowing whether the pressure you are feeling comes from external or internal sources is the first step to managing it. Use the Table in the previous section as a guide. Is it one of those 80% self-generated *What If* stresses that have not yet happened, are not real, that you can do nothing about right now anyway. If so, relax, maybe laugh and dismiss it from your mind.

Is the tension you feel the result of a single stress or of several? Allowing several stresses to accumulate makes tackling them insurmountable. Persons almost always feel 'stressed out' as the result of a stress buildup. The solution is to identify what the components are. Write them down. There are always one or two stress-causing issues that can be dealt with easily. Get them over with. Once they are out of the way your stress pile looks a little smaller.

What can you tackle next? How many stressors are caused by worrying about something beyond your control? How many can you postpone or, even better, dismiss? Get over long-standing issues such as bearing a grudge, feeling betrayed, ignored or neglected by someone who did not call or forgot your birthday. Did someone ask an intrusive question? There may be no malice in their action. If it is work-related you may be able to get some help. Seek advice if you need it. Your peers will love to be asked. You are allowed to "fail" occasionally. There is no shame in that.

As the old saying goes, it's not how many times you fall down, it's how many times you get up that counts. Learn to say "No" sometimes. You cannot do everything nor help every-body. If you are upset with someone or they upset you, talk to them. Stewing over whatever it is does not do you any good, neither does feeling guilty. These are a waste of time, emotion and energy.

Coping Skills

The more often you cope well with difficult situations, the bet-ter you manage. Astronauts analyze the coping techniques they have been using and, if necessary, learn how to modify them to confront stress more effectively. As part of the US collaboration with the Russians, training involved being parachuted into the Siberian wild in the middle of winter and having to fend for themselves for several days. They needed creativity to survive and find their way to shelter. This reinforces self-confidence.

Make a Difference

Your brain can perceive the same situation as a threat, a commonplace event, or a thrill. Perception makes all the difference to how your body responds.

For instance, pain, which is considered a stress, can be relieved either by medication or by a placebo, a substance that contains no active drugs. But for the placebo to work, the brain has to believe in its power. A recent study on the value of arthroscopic knee surgery (the use of an endoscope to inspect the inside of a joint) showed that pain was relieved just as effectively for patients who only underwent placebo procedures as it did for those who received the full surgery.

Give Happiness

The great songwriters Betty Comden and Adolph Green got it right when they wrote, "Make someone happy . . . and you will be happy too."

Turning the focus away from our own problems and onto lending someone else a hand can be the key to easing our stress and enjoying the warm glow of knowing we have made a difference in the world. Whether it is a troubled family member, a lonely neighbor, a friend coping with a loss, or a stranger at your local food pantry, try setting aside a little time each day to do a good turn for someone or to send a good thought their way.

Be Grateful

As we were growing up, mother constantly reminded my sister and me to be grateful. In our case, it was mostly for the wonderful father we had whose work made it possible for us to have a first-rate education. Remember the pious Victorian heroine, Pollyanna, who was continually finding something to be thankful for in every bad turn of events? It turns out that the age-old advice to count your blessings really works, according to University of Pennsylvania psychology professor Martin Seligman and others who have pioneered the "positive psychology" movement. More recent research has expanded the evidence of the powerful connection of gratitude to happiness.

Gratitude boosts your health. It increases self-esteem, improves sleep and raises energy levels. Dr. Robert Emmons at UC Davis says "Without gratitude, life can be lonely, depressing and impoverished. Gratitude enriches human life. It elevates, energizes, inspires and transforms. People are moved, made aware and humbled through expressions of gratitude. Gratitude has been shown to make people more compassionate. In doing so they become more forgiving, they let go of their own problems, they are less depressed and anxious, sleep better, have fewer headaches and migraines, feel more empathy towards others and feel more socially connected.

How do you want to feel? By consciously thinking every morning of five things you are grateful for, keeping a gratitude journal, saying thank you or sending thank you notes or e-mails or a note of appreciation, you become more aware of others' problems. You count your blessings and become more inclined to help.

In studying the factors that lead to happiness — or "subjective well-being" —cultivating a habitual "attitude of gratitude" has been found to be the best thing you can do for yourself and your happiness.

Help your 50+ loved ones

Stress for the older age groups is about how to be taken care of. For the earlier age brackets stress is about taking care of others. The best solution is ideally to make it a lifetime mutual stress relief habit so that it becomes second nature.

Modern families that live near each other and interact physically and daily are the exception. Modern technologies accentuate the dissociation between parents and children and grandchildren. There is no eye contact, touching hugging in social media. There is nothing social about them. Even the telephone that depended on voice is being replaced by texting. Unfortunately younger generations have never known it otherwise. The harm done that depriving such daily stimulation of the senses as a stress has not been established yet. Even the most considerate and loving younger family members must feel that staying in touch by texting is the norm. Yet I doubt that any calming serotonin or oxytocin is generated.

Equally for the older generations it is stressful to be forced into the electronic age, deprived of the benefits of hearing, smelling, touching, hugging — all of which stimulate calming, nurturing reactions.

What can be done until social media can incorporate appropriate sensory stimulation into everyday devices. Skype provides visual and hearing cues and is a start. In the meantime nothing can replace physical interaction. Make a point of spending as much time with your older or younger loved ones, on a one on one basis so that the benefit is not diluted and impersonal. Annual holiday gatherings may be catch up but not the time to truly share. Go for a walk or travel on a one on one basis that is mutually fun and a source of discovery. Tell them about yourself; share secret likes, desires, build trust. Ask for their help. Show your vulnerability. Write your life stories if you are older; seek the opinion of your younger family members. Share your stress worries; seek each other's advice. Make the relationship special, not a duty. And above all do not whine.

Stop Worrying

You can avoid stressful situations up to a certain point. To prevent sunburn, you stay out of the sun. If you find driving stressful, don't drive at night, during the rush hour or on icy roads. Get going earlier in the morning to avoid the rush hour. Worrying about some impending disaster over which you have no control causes unnecessary stress and anxiety.

When living in California, I had to straighten the pictures on my office walls every morning, because small earth tremors happened all the time and put the pictures askew. I soon accepted this as a simple fact of life, but some of my neighbors moved away. They were paralyzed with worry about when the next big earthquake might hit.

Another classic example of self-generated stress comes from believing rumors and worrying about things that may never happen. During the thirty-two years I worked at NASA, my department was reorganized more than fourteen times. Rumors of pending reorganizations were therefore constantly circulating. Paying attention to them could freeze one's ability to function as indeed happened to some. Their work and health both suffered and all they could do all day was to discuss the rumors.

What Is the Worst Thing That Can Happen

This is not a bad exercise to do though it might appear to diminish the seriousness of the event. You forgot to send that special birthday card. You missed an appointment. You did not take your pill. If you are still alive it cannot have been that serious.

There are certain stresses you cannot avoid. That earthquake shook you up and the house may have crumbled. Did it? Were you insured? You stay up nights worrying about the next one. Are you prepared with the right latches on your cupboards and taking fragile things off shelves? You have no way of knowing when or where the next rumble will come. Moving elsewhere does not guarantee safety from Mother Nature — the risk of earthquake may be less, but there are hurricanes, tornadoes, floods, blizzards, mud slides, sink holes. Accept these risks as part of the price we pay for all the wonders of life on Earth.

Think, then Act

To make progress in managing stress, you should first pause, count to ten, take a few deep breaths, push your shoulders down, relax your jaw, and analyze what it is that is worrying you. Is there something you can do about it? If not, worrying about it is only a waste of energy.

Do Something

Most importantly, to manage stress, you should take action. The best action is to remove the cause of the stress, but even a diversion, such as taking exercise, can be effective. Most of the stress we suffer is psychological and therefore manageable.

Your brain initiates your stress response in the first place. It should be equally capable of managing the stress response as well.

Exercise your brain. A healthier brain with lots of active neurons and synaptic connections is more likely to learn new coping skills than a sluggish brain. The brain loves novelty so take up a new hobby, learn how to paint, play the piano, a new language, or start a collection of semi-precious or even precious gems if you can afford them. If you are right-handed use your left hand to eat or garden. Play. Get good at Sudoku or learn a new sport. Take a different route on your walk or to the store. To reprogram your coping skills you are asking your brain to take a different way. Watch how others cope. Do anything that will prevent your brain from doing something automatically.

Make Lists

Identifying the real source of a problem and then realistically sizing it up goes a long way towards resolving it.

Write down every possible thing that is bothering you. Look at the list, item by item. You will find that you can dismiss some worries as unfounded. Are you worrying about something that may not happen? No amount of worrying is going to change the outcome. Cross it off.

Some world event or tragedy you heard on the news has you worried? Perhaps there is a small way to help by sending off a letter or a donation. If you can, do so, and you will feel better. Otherwise, cross it off. Accentuate the positive.

Attitude

Think of coping with stress as play, as a puzzle to solve, a game. Older people tend to see themselves in a negative light, based on feelings and behaviors they attribute to aging. If they drop something, or forget a name they are quick to say, "How foolish of me" or "I can't do anything right."

Make a list of your positive and negative thoughts or statements especially the positive ones. "I cannot do anything right" should be challenged by several positive statements of things you always do right. This holds true at any age. See the glass as half full rather than half empty, and you will live a healthier, happier life.

Goals

If you have a long-term goal you are more likely to reach it with small, controllable steps. Make sure every day includes one or two things, however trivial, that you are sure you can accomplish. Write a letter, call a friend, or read ten pages of a book. At the end of the day you can look back and say, "I did x and y rather than be overpowered by statements like "I have so much to do."

Control

Diverting attention to something you can control is another way of keeping calm. Stewing over how much you lost in the stock market dive of recent years is a waste of energy and can make you feel low. But how much did you really lose when you compare the current value of the stock not with its peak price but with what you paid for it in the first place? And do you still have the things that really matter — good health, family, a job, and a roof over your head?

Successes

For those able to move, be reasonably active or exercise. The most obvious benefit is the relief of anxiety. Those who have an active lifestyle, move about all day, are calmer, less angry or tense, happier, and better sleepers. Reducing your sitting time, interrupting it with getting up and generally moving about can improve immune function, too. It is particularly effective for people who suffer from low-level anxiety. And it's a lot cheaper than anti-anxiety drugs. However, if you are taking pills do not give them up before first checking with your doctor.

If you do not already exercise, you can add that to your overall moving activities but start slowly. Set a pace that is beyond a shuffle and enough to raise a sweat. Do your exercises standing up rather than sitting down. Find some steps you can climb. If all you can do at first is stand up several times that is a great beginning. Can you squat and stand holding onto the sink at first. Intersperse your exercises throughout the day or go to the gym on a regular basis. The more days a week the better, but start with three times a week, allowing time to recover.

Do not expect immediate changes in your anxiety symptoms. You do not get rapid results with drugs either. Do not start out by setting yourself unreasonable goals: that will only increase your anxiety. Wear comfortable shoes and loose clothes, and equip yourself with your favorite music or radio program. As with other stimuli, you are more likely to stick with exercise, and it will be more beneficial, if you vary it.

Although most experts agree that aerobic exercise, being active all-day long is probably your best approach. Getting up from your chair may seem insignificant but for others it is an achievement and the road to independence. Sitting back down slowly without collapsing into a seat is a challenge for most of us. Achieve it and you are reinforcing those self-confidence brain programs.

Manage Time

Time pressures are an example of self-imposed stress. Judy Weinberg says, "The trouble with seniors — too much to do." Time management is the best way of reducing the stress of anxiety. We all know one person who weaves through the traffic believing he or she will get to their destination faster, only to find that they are stopped by the merciless traffic lights. This is enough to send stress hormones pouring through their veins. Here is a great opportunity to practice breathing deeply, drop your shoulders and your jaw — you will easily make up the 45 seconds later.

Things we "should do" seem to creep up on us, until they become overwhelming. I have found that my favorite practice of list-making comes to the rescue. Writing down what "I should do" is not only a memory jog. But when the job has been carried out, I have the satisfaction of crossing it off the list.

At the start of each day, make a mental note of what you would like to accomplish: make telephone calls, exercise, go to the cleaners, pick up groceries, visit a sick friend or an exhibition. Whatever the task on the list, allow at least fifteen minutes more than you expect it to take. Then you will not become frantic if you start to fall behind.

Any time you try telephoning a public company these days, you have to talk to a machine, and you will almost inevitably find that it takes longer than you expected to get through to the person you want.

Probably the most valuable training I ever got at NASA was on a time-management course. I learned how to organize the day into hourly chunks, accept no calls during each 45 minute block of undisturbed time. This allowed me to make headway on some task. I would then return calls during the 15 minute pause. Those who called quickly learned that their calls would be answered.

Another stress-reducing time management trick I practiced at the office was to review the tasks ahead before the day started. Usually people start with the biggest job that is likely to be the most time-consuming and stressful. Using this approach you might finish the day empty-handed without completing a single thing, then having to work late or take work home. Instead, start first with the simplest task that you know you can finish. This will give you the sense of accomplishment and satisfaction to move on to the more burdensome jobs feeling calmer and in control.

Avoid Stress-Emitters: Befriend Stress Relievers

Reduce your stress level by giving a wide berth to anxious people who unload their stress onto others. They generally end up feeling better as a result of sharing their woes. Or have you noticed how you may dread answering the phone when this one person calls late at night talking incessantly with negative news? By the time they have unloaded their problems onto you, you are wide awake while they happily get a good night's sleep. You know exactly whom I am talking about. Think of them as being infected with a stress virus you do not want to catch. Keep your distance to stay healthy. If you want to keep them as a friend let them know that you cannot talk to them right then but if they would call next morning at 9a.m. you could give them your undivided attention.

Just as there are stress-emitters there are stress-relievers. Have you noticed how relaxed you are, how much you enjoy being with some people, and not others? These are persons who allow you to relax and be yourself. Usually they end up being friends because you feel you can call on them whenever you need support.

Time seems to fly as we get older. We never seem to have enough time to do everything. Making lists, being selective, saying "No", rejecting wasteful anxiety, goes a long way towards freeing up more time and living a low-stress-lifestyle.

Support Network

This is probably the most effective and easiest form of coping. Surrounding yourself with people you like and can rely on is a most powerful way of providing protection from the harmful effects of stress.

The emphasis here is on support, not just social activities. I find cocktail parties with lots of people I do not know stressful; others may not. Gauge who you can socialize with to find emotional reward. You may have a good social network on the job but if you work from home or are retired you will need to work at building up a social network. Living in the country can leave you isolated. Organize a once-a-week meeting at a local restaurant, the library or join the gardening club. Talk to the people behind the counter or in the queue. Some find it difficult to smile but soon they will soften and appreciate your warmth. They probably need you more than you need them. Stay in touch with friends. Many use the computer as a social vehicle, but nothing beats the personal touch.

People involved in warm, loving relationships are likely to live longer, healthier lives. Research has even shown that sociable people are the least likely to catch a cold. In contrast to general assumptions, the New England Centenarian Study found that instead of being abandoned and alone, centenarians had strong family ties and many close friends. Madame Marie Simrova of Calgary, when 103, had a strong circle of younger friends "mostly because my contemporaries had died." It gave her the incentive to dress up and look as elegant as she always did. A circle of close friends does not just happen. She worked at developing and keeping these younger friends, and they enjoyed learning from her.

Loneliness or being alone? Some people enjoy their own company and need time on their own to properly relax. In contrast, others find it stressful. Social isolation, the stress of being alone or feeling alone even in a crowd, without close friends or family, increases anxiety and seems to trigger signals in the body that suppress the immune system, increasing the risk of sickness and earlier death. Social isolation is very hard to take, even by very well adjusted and highly trained people, such as astronauts and cosmonauts, who know what they are in for.

Valery Palyakov, the Russian cosmonaut who in 1994-95 set the record for the longest time in space (14 months), said afterwards: "It's a real effort to be away from everything. I mean, you are really isolated. They talk about the French Foreign Legion. This is really.... you're in the Sahara Desert, and there's just no way around it."

Studies have shown that people who have a heart attack and are unmarried or lack emotional support are three times more likely to have a relapse than those who are not isolated in this way. And they die much sooner. John Cacioppo at the University of Chicago sees isolation as a health risk at any age, comparable to smoking and obesity. His group studied 2,632 undergraduate students. They found that even in a crowd there were some who found it difficult to make connections. They felt lonely even though they were not alone, and they had higher cortisol levels in the morning and throughout the day. "Lonely people view the world as a more threatening place," he commented. These observations emphasize the difference between "being alone" and "feeling lonely."

Get a Pet

Owning a pet is something akin to having a child or another dependent. Make sure you made arrangements for someone willing to take over your pet if your health should fail or the pet has to go into a shelter for homeless animals. Should you no longer be able to care for your pet, it might be abandoned. It could be very stressful for both of you.

Preferably, get a pet you can hug or stroke, like a cat or dog, or at least one you can talk to, like a canary or budgerigar. People who own dogs live longer. This may be true for cat-owners and those who keep other pets. Dogs show their unconditional affection by wagging their tail or licking you and they instinctively know when you need comforting. They offer protection and make you feel less vulnerable. They can sense when you are not feeling well and look at you with empathy. Dogs have an important added advantage. They make you take a walk at least twice a day. Going out and the exercise itself are invaluable.

If you do not want to own a pet, how about starting a dog-walking service for neighbors? You do not walk too well? You can do this at your own pace, on flat terrain. You may make some pocket money on the side and expand your social network as you improve your health. Many more people will stop to pat your dog and talk to you than when you are walking alone. Failing a pet, talking to your plants is known to have similar soothing, stress-reducing effects. Astronauts in space congregate around plant experiments because it makes them feel calmer.

Love, Sex

Reach out and touch somebody. The value of touching and hugging as part of social support and sensory therapy should not be underestimated. It's not just people who feel better after a hug. Dr. Orlaith Fraser at Liverpool's John Moores University studied chimps at Chester Zoo and found that hugs, strokes and kisses helped lower their stress levels.

He studied the behavior of chimps after fights over food, mates or seating arrangements. No sooner had the fight ended than like children who will put an arm around a friend's shoulder if they have been bullied, another chimp would approach the victim, wrap his arms around him or even kiss or groom him. Friends were the most likely to offer support.

Do you touch with the fingers or the whole hand? It makes a lot of difference to the soothing effectiveness of the touch. In Mediterranean and Latin American cultures, and in the days when we did not worry about sexual harassment, touching, patting someone's back or knee and walking arm in arm were perfectly normal — tacit indicators of social support.

Touch has important physiological benefits in its own right. Research among elderly populations at the University of Miami, School of Medicine found that those touched become more social, develop healthier habits, and get sick less often. People in loving relationships and happy marriages live longer. And for those young and old who believe sex isn't something older people are supposed to have, think again.

SEX AFTER 50

"Sex is about more than orgasms…. When you're older, you realize that sex is about the journey, not the destination. You enjoy exploring each other. Sexual confidence comes from finally being comfortable in your own skin regardless of the appearance of your body parts." ~ Erica Jagger, Huffington Post, July 3, 2015.

Sex has long been known as the ultimate stress relief. As long as you are able to, carry on making love.

And hug often. There is nothing like a warm hug to make you feel good; its healing power is very real. What's more, you can keep hugging long after sex fades.

Manage Menopause

Stressful thoughts and events causing anxiety or anger can trigger fast, shallow chest breathing. In most cases, one minute later you will experience the beginning sensations of a hot flash. Some 80% of American women tend to breathe in this anxiety-provoking, upper chest breathing and are more likely to experience hot flashes. In contrast, if you switch to slow deep diaphragmatic breathing throughout the day and interrupt every gasp with a moment of holding your breath, you will reduce anxiety-inducing fast shallow chest breathing and fewer or no hot flashes. Try it.

Defer

If you must worry save it for later. Worry is one area where procrastination can actually be productive! Put off worrying by exercising, going for a walk, playing tennis, or enjoying a few holes of golf. Go to a movie, a play, a concert, or an art gallery. Look for light, pleasant, amusing subjects. Take active breaks from work or irksome problems to give your brain a chance to reboot. Walking away from a problem may help you solve it. These activities give you a "time-out" from stress. Invite some friends or neighbors for a tea party. You may even be able to train yourself not to worry about things you can do nothing about.

Reward

Are you still worried about something and cannot get it off your mind? If you haven't pampered yourself in a while, maybe it's time for a treat. Reward yourself.

Have your hair done. Go to a spa. Soak in a jaccuzzi. Indulge in a massage. Buy a new necktie or something pretty. Spend time enjoying nature as often as you can. Have a glass of red wine (only one!). Surround yourself with pleasant ways of stimulating your senses. Buy some flowers or work in the garden. Sniff some herbs, fried onions, fresh roasted coffee or even freshly baked bread.

TURN INWARD

Become more aware. When in a dilemma we look for things to distract us rather than resolve the situation. Although you may be tempted to reach for a pill to ease anxiety it will not help you solve the problem. Your best approach is to turn inward and focus on yourself and your surroundings. What is happening to you and how are you reacting to it? Learn to actively relax and focus on your breathing and its rhythm.

Because so much of your mind is taken up with what you did and have to do, you might not pay enough attention on who you are, how you change and feel at any one moment. This takes training and practice until it becomes second nature. It does not happen overnight. You can then instantly be aware – be mindful – so that you are better able to calm your fears and anxieties wherever and whenever you need to. Replace them with feelings of love, compassion and gratitude.

Below I share information I feel equipped to describe and some particularly that you may find useful. They include in alphabetical order several Active Relaxation techniques including the Alexander technique, Biofeedback, breathing, whole body scan, hypnosis and self-hypnosis, the Relaxation Response, Yoga and MEDITATION

Energy psychology techniques such as the Emotional Freedom Technique (EFT), also known as Tapping, can be very effective in reducing anxiety. Information about these techniques can be found on web sites, your local wellness facility, senior center, YMCA, and local newspaper.

Meditation for even a few minutes a day can help relieve anxiety and chronic pain. With perseverance, it also can help with self-control, useful for breaking bad habits, like smoking and provide a sense of well-being.

Spend time in nature as often as you can and find time to meditate. Science shows that a walk in the woods rejuvenates our minds and improves our ability to pay attention and focus.

ACTIVE RELAXATION

Take a calming break. The secret to all relaxation techniques is practice, practice, practice, until it becomes a spontaneous habit, when you can invoke spontaneously the feeling of the calmer state.

On a visit to Samoa, I was surprised to see everything coming to a standstill at 6 P.M. at the ringing of a bell throughout the island. Most Samoans gathered home with the family and sat quietly or prayed for 10 minutes, after which they all went on their way.

This gave them the opportunity every day to get together with the family and take a pause from whatever they were doing — a wonderful custom.

Alexander Technique

Named after its inventor Frederick M Alexander, it was developed in the 1890s as a personal tool to relieve breathing problems and hoarseness during public speaking. He credited the technique with allowing him to pursue his passion for Shakespearean acting. Most other methods take it for granted that 'one's awareness of oneself' is accurate, whereas Alexander realized that a person who had been using himself wrongly for a long time could not trust his feelings (sensory appreciation) in carrying out any activity. Pain and distress arise from postural misalignment. It can be caused by repeated misuse of the body over a long period of time with one's weight unevenly distributed, holding one's head incorrectly during sitting, standing, walking or running. The purpose of the technique is to help people unlearn maladaptive physical habits and return to a balanced state of rest and poise in which the body is well-aligned — a prerequisite to total relaxation.

Breathe

Try whichever count, three or five, suits you best to help you slow down your normal breathing. Sit or stand comfortably with your belly softened. Breathe in for a slow count of three or five, hold it for another count of three or five, exhale slowly for a count of three or five and hold it for another count of three or five. You may vary the count as inhaling for a slow count of four, hold it for seven and exhale completely for eight. Repeat this breathing pattern three times and several times a day as needed. It is unobtrusive, and nobody can be any wiser. This type of breathing is useful to calm you down at any time, put you to sleep or preceding relaxation, hypnosis or meditation.

Antonio Sausys, author of *Yoga for Grief Relief* (2014) interviewed me for his TV show in California on Space and Healthy Aging. He says a simple way to bring awareness to the breath is to place the thumbs on the back of the ribs, close to the spine, with the fingers facing forward following the curve of your ribs. "To feel your ribs' breath, allow the ribs (and therefore the hands) to expand, moving away from the centre of the body as you inhale, and letting the ribs contract as you exhale, pressing them slightly towards the centre of the body with your hands at the end of the exhalation." He recommends this type of breathing to help people through the grieving process "to let go of everything that does not serve us, to fully exhale it al."

Massage

Massage, adjusted for age and condition, is increasingly recognized for its relaxing benefits to the mind and body. Try it with aromatic oils — chamomile or lavender is best — to a background of gentle soothing music. A study in ten healthy adults aged sixty-three to eighty-four published in 1998 in the Journal of Gerontology found it brought about improved immune function, better sleeping and eating patterns, and reduced anxiety and stress hormones.

BODY SCAN

Begin the day by practicing *a total body scan*. Not only is it relaxing but it instantly brings your attention to yourself and your body. I practice it in the morning before getting out of bed. "Good morning. How am I today?" You may surprise yourself. Or if you need a quick pick-me up, a body scan can help you any time of the day.

It takes very little time and gets you off to a good start. Lie on your back, palms up, eyes gently shut. Focus on your breath as it is happening, cool in, warm out. Begin with your feet. Feel their weight on the floor. Move up to your calves as they feel heavier, drawn through the floor by gravity. Then feel the weight of your thighs relaxing against the floor. Take your time. Move up to your hips and abdomen sinking down, then your chest, your arms and hands and last your heavy head. Let go.

Airports and workplaces now offer neck and shoulder massage. Many nursing facilities include shoulder, hand, and foot massage once a week. For those who can afford it, whole body massage is very beneficial. It improves circulation to the muscles and reduces muscle cramps and swelling around joints. However, make sure you talk to your doctor first if you have osteoporosis, blood clots, diabetes, cancer, or other conditions the massage therapist needs to know about.

Biofeedback

This is a relaxation technique that enables you to lower your blood pressure or heart rate by observing them on a display screen. It involves the use of equipment that allows you to watch on a screen what is happening to your heart rate or blood pressure. Simply concentrating on the figures and willing them to come down is sufficient to bring them down. Some people can do this in just one lesson. You can do it even without a screen.

Popular electronic devices like the *Fitbit biofeedback* and its modern equivalent *Muse* or *Apple Watch* are examples of simple ways you can have instant feedback of what your body is doing. It is also fun to use to train your heart rate to decrease at will when you feel stressed.

Hypnosis

This is a state of increased awareness that allows you to refocus your mind-set by making positive affirmations to yourself. Well-known hypnotist Dr. Susan Hepburn set up her practice in London to treat stressed-out workers in the 'square mile', the London financial district. Her practice has expanded to New York and Los Angeles. She treats persons who want to give up addictive behaviors, drugs, alcohol, smoking, obesity, as well as stress anxiety and a range of fears.

I was introduced to self-hypnosis when I was widowed and found it useful as a relaxation technique. Self-hypnosis uses mental imaging. Try to see yourself in your mind's eye relaxing, sinking into the floor, or wading into warm, soothing water or into the warm water on a sandy beach. With this comes mental relaxation.

Relaxation Technique

In 1975 Dr. Herbert Benson, a Boston cardiologist, was the first to introduce simple relaxation techniques to the US. In his book *The Relaxation Technique*, he outlined in simple terms the beneficial effects of using mind-over-body techniques to help you relax, in order to lower your heart rate or blood pressure. It's a matter of willing your heart rate or your blood pressure to come down. This is not the restricted province of hermits on the banks of the Ganges River.

The relaxation response slows your heartbeat and breathing, reduces oxygen consumption and offers a state of deep relaxation. According to Dr. Benson "The relaxation response is a state of deep rest that changes the physical and emotional responses to stress." His studies have shown that people can evoke this response and lessen the effects of stressful thoughts, by repeating a prayer, a word, sound, phrase or muscular activity.

Have you noticed how your blood pressure is higher when you have it taken at your doctor's office. I practice lowering my blood pressure every time I go the doctor for my physical by visualizing it dropping in my mind's eye. My blood pressure is normally low but it irks me that it is always slightly higher at the doctor's office. Try it. You can practice this relaxation technique to bring it down while waiting for the nurse to come and take it. You will probably realize that you are pushing your shoulders slightly down and concentrating on breathing out more than when you breathe in.

Yoga

Yoga is not exercise. It is a practice. Of all the practices you can join you will get most benefit from Yoga. First, you will learn how to get the most out of breathing correctly. Stretch your ligaments and tendons, your muscles and joints, feel calm and strong. And you will learn how to relax. Of these meditation and yoga are by far the most effective ways of producing a sense of calm. Why is this so? Because at the core of most anxiety attacks is holding your breath.

When you are anxious, the diaphragm freezes, does not move air downward as you breathe in, which means that your breath is shallow, and you don't get enough oxygen. This state sends a danger signal to your brain which perpetuates your state of anxiety. Your breathing quickens and becomes even more shallow. In turn it can lead to a panic attack when you may hyperventilate. And as the carbon dioxide levels drop, the hyperventilation makes the anxiety worse, causing fear. You may feel like you are having a heart attack or a stroke. Unless you can slow your breathing down, instinct will tell you to keep up the fast-pacing panting. That's why we say to someone who seems physically distressed, "Calm down and take some deep breaths." Anxiety builds up over the years.

The National Cancer Institute published guidelines from a study (H Greelee et al 2014) comparing the use of integrative therapies to support breast cancer patients. Data from 203 out of a total of 4900 articles were analyzed. Meditation, yoga and relaxation with imagery were recommended for routine use for common conditions including anxiety and mood disorders; these got an A grade. Stress management, yoga, massage, music therapy, and meditation were recommended for stress reduction, anxiety, depression, fatigue and quality of life (B grade). Many other interventions had weaker or no benefit.

Yoga and yoga breathing not only calms down anxiety and fear but reduces blood pressure in patients with hypertension. It reduces blood sugar levels in diabetics, cholesterol levels and body weight, corrects disturbed sleep, all of which result from poorly managed stress. Yoga particularly has psychological benefits for older people. Bohner and Tenenbaum (2014) compared sitting yoga with sitting exercise in persons 65 to 92 and found substantial benefits of chair yoga in anxiety, depression, well-being and a general sense of self-sufficiency in daily living. Interestingly, they found that it was their sense of self-control that primarily influenced their overall psychological health.

ENERGY PSYCHOLOGY

Emotional Freedom Technique (EFT)

EFT was popularized by Nick Ortner who developed scripts for specific subjects about which a person might be anxious and wanted to address. By making it practical and accessible, together with clever marketing, EFT has become useful as a quick tool in reducing anxiety by a type of 'reprogramming' circuitry – correcting bioelectrical short-circuiting that causes body reactions without adverse side–effects. EFT consists of tapping on meridians while addressing out loud whatever is making you anxious and unhappy followed by positive assertions. Meridians are found at the top of your scalp, around eye sockets, upper lip, under clavicle, underarm rib-cage, and the outer part of your hand above the little finger.

You can think of EFT as a psychological acupressure, based on the same traditional acupuncture energy meridians used for over 5,000 years to treat physical and emotional disorders, but without needles. Since being reviewed by the American Psychological Association in 2012 in the Journal of General Psychology, EFT has moved closer to becoming accepted as an evidence-based treatment.

Among its benefits, EFT research has shown that it increases positive emotions, hope and enjoyment, decreasing negative ones, including fear and anxiety. You can teach yourself how to use EFT; or as with hypnosis or acupuncture, if you have a serious problem or habit you want to solve, make sure you get a properly trained EFT practitioner. It can make all the difference.

MEDITATION

Meditation is not just another relaxation technique. By now pretty much all of us know that meditation provides many benefits, including reduced tension and stress. It is a state of greater awareness as you focus inward on the present. It involves sitting relaxed, breathing gently, and calming the mind by emptying it of thought, allowing thoughts to pass by, concentrating on or contemplating just one thing – your breathing, humming, a word.

Meditation is a proven stress-management technique. Studies with Tibetan Buddhist monks have shown remarkable changes in calming the cardiovascular system, boosting immune function and controlling body temperature even when sitting in extremely cold weather.

Neuroscientists have shown that meditation can change brain chemistry. Dr. Richard Davidson and colleagues at the University of Wisconsin found that meditation induced changes in the level of brain waves associated with learning and conscious perception. It thickens the cortex where we make decisions, analyze, feel more connected to others and dream. You start to live for now rather than for what's next, dwell on what just happened, may happen, anticipating the future. Neither is real and meditation helps you focus on the present.

Take a brain break with three simple steps. Sit cross-legged on the floor, a pillow or a chair. Let your belly soften. Take three deep breaths and exhale completely and slowly. Now focus on breathing normally and relaxing your shoulders. When thoughts arise, let them go like clouds passing by. Be patient. Notice that your breathing and heart rate will slow down, your shoulders drop, your jaw relax and your stress will eventually melt away. Build up to meditating 10-15 minutes a day and several times a day if you can; or even take a short 5-minute meditation break at your desk or during lunch as a time-out. If you go for a walk try walking-meditation where you walk as slowly as you possibly can concentrating on observing where and how your foot strikes the ground and moves you forward.

Centers for teaching meditation for stress reduction are now springing up everywhere. The best known and those that have been around longest are the Center for Mindfulness Stress Reduction (MBSR) pioneered 30 years ago by

Dr. John Kabat-Zin at the University of Massachusetts, Medical School, in Boston MA, and the Center for Mindfulness Stress Reduction created by Dr Jeffrey Brantley a psychiatrist at Duke University in Durham NC. There are now many others.

The benefits of meditation are countless. Research is showing that it can help in depression, memory loss, changes gene expression and makes vaccines and administered medications more effective. Meditation was found to increase blood flow to the brain and reverse memory loss in patients with memory problems. A Harvard study has found that it literally rebuilds your brain's gray matter in just 8 weeks. And a 5-year study published in *Circulation* (Schneider et al 2012) found a 48% reduction in heart attacks, stroke and death in 210 persons using meditation.

This is early times in research on how meditation works with much more to come as it becomes part of mainstream therapeutics.

REFLECTIONS

Having read the chapter, complete these brief but important contemplations to jump start your journey to greater well-being:

- Identify three things you now recognize you regularly do that help manage stress:
    1.
    2.
    3.

- Which instant relief techniques can you start using to-day? _____

  _____

- What long-term strategies do you want to add to your tool kit? _____

  _____

SIX | Making Choices

We have explored what stress is, and how to relate to it in a way that allows us to live the best life once past age 50. Living a happier life as you live longer is more possible than you probably can imagine.

Each decade brings new stresses but also wisdom and better attitude. Perhaps you are going through a particular challenge that has not been addressed. If so, apply the wisdom and tools in this book to best deal with it in a practical way.

You have realized that we each have a threshold of stress tolerance and the good news is that you can raise this threshold so that you don't let stress overwhelm you. The higher the threshold, the greater your peace of mind, the better you will handle stress. You can raise the threshold with better health and more effective coping habits.

Read over something that resonated with you. Don't wait. Test yourself. If you skipped the *Reflections* at the end of each chapter, go through them now.

Remember, stress is not something that happens to you but something that happens in you. What you feel inside is a stimulus or a strain depending on how your brain interprets what's happening. How do you feel? How do you want to feel? Stress fills you with feelings – excitement, love of life or pain, fear, living under pressure and despair. Take your choice, are you to be stimulated or damaged? To not manage your stress is a quiet killer: the resulting inflammation and oxidation will make you sick. Every cell in your body is affected.

The secret to living life well is to *adapt to stress* – to maintain or regain balance. Enjoy the best; skillfully dodge the worst. Few of us can do this spontaneously - adaptation has to be learned.

Ignore advice that tells you to 'bust' stress or promises you a 'stress-free life.' There is no such thing. Reading this book you will have realized by now that stress is a normal, necessary part of living. Yet like anything in excess it becomes a negative. The big secret that is mostly missed is that it's all about keeping stress under tabs and not wiping it away. It's like a bottle of champagne. It's the right amount of bubbles that make us love it. It's about attitude, mind-set, keeping that stimulus, those stress bubbles contained but popping.

Life beyond 50 is a time of discovery, of opportunities. It is different from our first 50 years because we have so many experiences behind us. We can tap into our accumulated wisdom. As people are now living longer we are given bonus time to enjoy the best of years. Family, love, sex, partnerships, work, children, parents, learning, fun, friends all must be juggled with minimum strain. Set aside regular time to look inward and pause, lest the stress roller-coaster leads you astray. If it all gets too much for you seek help.

Reflecting on how life after 50 could be and what brought you to this point should help you establish a spring-board: you now know that stress is not the demon it's been made out to be. You know how it works. Life can be challenging. You are now more aware that your reactions and feelings are not abnormal. You will have greater control than you thought possible over what happens or 'when things happen to you'. Stop, step back, breathe deeply, and use those stages where you learned to check stress before it piles up. Try some of the approaches outlined in the Tool-Kit that work best for you.

Almost immediately you will recognize that you are steadily changing your Data Base with experiences that you rely on to guide your reactions. Positive thoughts and feelings, gratitude and compassion will more regularly supplant anxiety, anger or sadness. It will be easier to see the funny side, to cry, shrug it off, laugh.

Savor life. Think about feeling well. Do you feel joyful, loved, loving, trusted, connected, generous, grateful? Studies now show that practicing feeling gratitude makes you a happier more compassionate person. Choose a time, maybe every morning, to say thank you for the day, for being alive. Reach up and stretch. Focus on the good things. You will immediately feel better.

Shrug off problems. People who accept change know how to forgive and let things go. Do not stew over frustrations you can do nothing about.

With stress apparently responsible for or aggravating 80% of chronic diseases, take matters in your own hands. You have the opportunity that age gives you, the wisdom and the tools. Enjoy a better, longer life, while getting wealthy by saving on medical bills.

How do you get started in the first place? Get your toe in the water right now by experiencing a reward however small, perhaps a second of calm. I suggest you begin by dropping your jaw. Smile. Even laugh. *Feel* the relief even in the most stressful conditions, whether at work or maybe caring for someone. Enjoy the feeling. Try it again and again even when you do not think you are stressed.

I am dropping my jaw as I write these words. It feels playful, silly. Then I stretch my arms up high while smiling at myself. Join me. That was easy! Then once you enjoy that sensation routinely, try another one; maybe a forced exhalation while waiting at the traffic light. Check it in the Tool-kit under breathing.

Well done! You're on your way to coming to terms with your stress. You're in control. Relief, happiness, calm, smiles await you. It's your life. Becoming aware of how you feel and how you think enables you to make better choices. You can choose happiness just as you can choose unhappiness. Bring wisdom to your choices. No one can do it for you. Enjoy life over 50. I recommend it!

About the Author

Joan Vernikos, PhD is a pioneering medical research scientist who has conducted seminal studies in space medicine, inactivity physiology, stress and healthy aging.

Recruited by NASA in 1964 to study the stress on astronauts during space launch, she later worked on ways to keep astronauts healthy in the weightlessness of space and upon re-introduction to earth's gravity. Vernikos served as Life Sciences Director at the NASA Ames Research Center, CA, from 1986 to 1993 and NASA Director of Life Sciences at HQ from 1993 to 2000.

Winner of numerous awards, and recognition by peers, member of the International Academy of Astronautics, Vernikos was inducted into its Hall of Fame in 2018. Author of the groundbreaking "Sitting Kills, Moving Heals - How Everyday Movement Will Prevent Pain, Illness and Early Death, and Exercise Alone Won't," her mission is to empower individuals to greater control of their health and well-being through frequent daily movement, and effective stress management.

Made in the USA
Columbia, SC
01 November 2018